Essential
Algarve

by Christopher Catling

Christopher Catling has written more than 30 travel guides. He is a regular contributor to travel magazines on the Internet and in print. His books on London, Florence, Venice and Amsterdam are inspired by a keen interest in art and architecture, whilst his love of the countryside is reflected in guides to Madeira, Umbria and Crete.

Above: *the beach at Carvoeiro*

AA Publishing

BARCO RABELO

Above: *typical* azulejo

Front cover: *Armação de Pêra; girl wearing lace; tiles at Albufeira*
Back cover: *display of colourful gourds*

Written by Christopher Catling

Produced by AA Publishing.
© The Automobile Association 1999
Maps © The Automobile Association 1999

Distributed in the United Kingdom by AA Publishing, Norfolk House, Priestley Road, Basingstoke, Hampshire, RG24 9NY.

A CIP catalogue record for this book is available from the British Library.

ISBN 0 7495 1901 0

Published by AA Publishing, a trading name of Automobile Association Developments Limited, whose registered office is Norfolk House, Priestley Road, Basingstoke, Hampshire, RG24 9NY.
Registered number 1878835.

Colour separation: Pace Colour, Southampton
Printed and bound in Italy by Printer Trento srl

Find out more about AA Publishing and the wide range of services the AA provides by visiting our Web site at www.theaa.co.uk

Contents

About this Book 4

About this Book

KEY TO SYMBOLS

🗺️ map reference to the maps found in the What to See section (see below)

✉️ address or location

☎️ telephone number

🕐 opening times

🍴 restaurant or café on premises or near by

Ⓜ️ nearest underground train station

🚌 nearest bus/tram route

🚉 nearest overground train station

⛴️ ferry crossings and boat excursions

✈️ travel by air

ℹ️ tourist information

♿ facilities for visitors with disabilities

✋ admission charge

↔️ other places of interest near by

❓ other practical information

▶ indicates the page where you will find a fuller description

---

Essential *Algarve* is divided into five sections to cover the most important aspects of your visit to the Algarve.

Viewing the Algarve pages 5–14
An introduction to the Algarve by the author.
The Algarve's Features
Essence of the Algarve
The Shaping of the Algarve
Peace and Quiet
The Algarve's Famous

Top Ten pages 15–26
The author's choice of the Top Ten places to see in the Algarve, listed in alphabetical order, each with practical information.

What to See pages 27–90
The four main areas of the Algarve, each with its own brief introduction and an alphabetical listing of the main attractions.
Practical information
Snippets of 'Did you know...' information
5 suggested walks
4 suggested tours
2 features

Where To... pages 91–116
Detailed listings of the best places to eat, stay, shop, take the children and be entertained.

Practical Matters pages 117–24
A highly visual section containing essential travel information.

Maps
All map references are to the individual maps found in the What to See section of this guide.
For example, the village of Estói has the reference 🗺️ 29E2 – indicating the page on which the map is located and the grid square in which the village is to be found. A list of the maps that have been used in this travel guide can be found in the index.

Prices
Where appropriate, an indication of the cost of an establishment is given by **£** signs: **£££** denotes higher prices, **££** denotes average prices, while **£** denotes lower charges.

Star Ratings
Most of the places described in this book have been given a separate rating:

✪✪✪   Do not miss
✪✪   Highly recommended
✪   Worth seeing

Viewing the Algarve

Above: *watching and waiting*
Right: *bringing home the catch*

Christopher Catling's Algarve

Traditional boats are still used to fish for tuna, cod and sardines

When I first visited the Algarve in the 1970s, Portugal was only just opening its doors to the world, having finally shrugged off a dictatorship that had clung on to power since 1932. Keen to catch up with the rest of Europe, Portugal leapt in a decade from the Middle Ages to the post-industrial age, and the freedoms that came in the wake of the revolution resulted in the Algarve's rapid development.

A quarter of a century on, the Algarve is firmly on the map as a rewarding and inexpensive holiday destination. Fortunately, it has managed to achieve this without destroying the features that make it so special. Whole swathes of the Algarve remain delightfully wild and unexploited, with scores of little bays and coves where you can laze the day away if you choose, while the endless expanses of golden sand further east allow everyone to stake out their own private beach territory.

Perhaps the most attractive feature of the Algarve is simply that it combines so many different attractions – beaches, luxurious hotels and manicured golf-courses, nightlife and sunshine. Equally, the Algarve satisfies my taste for exploring churches, slipping into centuries-old hilltowns to observe the way of life, or rambling gently along cliff paths and through orange-scented groves, enjoying the wild flowers and butterflies.

Integration

The Algarvian readiness to embrace all comers is part of a tradition of tolerance dating back many centuries. Many of the Jews expelled from Spain in 1492 by the Catholic monarchs Ferdinand and Isabella found a new home in the Algarve, and the region's architecture, cooking, ceramics and agriculture all result from the absorption of North African and Spanish settlers and their cultural influences.

The Algarve's Features

Geography

• The Algarve, Portugal's southernmost province, is separated from the Alentejo, the next province north, by a range of low mountains known as the Serra de Monchique to the west and the Serra do Caldeirão to the east.

• To the west and south the region is bounded by the Atlantic Ocean, and to the east the River Guadiana forms the frontier between Portugal and Andalucia (Spain).

• The Algarve represents about one-twentieth of Portugal's total area (4,960sq km) and measures about 135km east to west and between 27 and 50km north to south.

Landscape

• Topographically, the Algarve divides into three main regions: the coast (*litoral*), where most of the intensive tourist development is located; the foothills (*barrocal*), where most of the agriculture is concentrated; and the almost uninhabited mountains (*serra*), which support extensive cork oak forests.

• The Algarve includes mainland Europe's southwest-ernmost point, the legendary Cabo de São Vicente (Cape St Vincent). The western end of the coast is composed of eroded sandstone cliffs of many colourful hues, with numerous marine grottoes and wind-eroded rock stacks, while towards the east the coast is flat and sandy, with long beaches and barrier islands forming shallow lagoons.

Climate

• The mountains separating the Algarve from the Alentejo also shelter it from cold continental air in winter, so that the region's winter climate is markedly milder than the rest of Portugal, though it does have high rainfall, due to Atlantic fronts.

• The coast is traditionally divided into the *barlavento* (windward) region (from Cape St Vincent to Albufeira), which bears the brunt of the southwesterly winds, and the more sheltered *sotavento* (leeward).

Exports

Portugal is the world's biggest producer of cork, and much of it is grown in the Algarve and the Alentejo. Traditional almond and fig production, while still important, is in decline, but citrus production is increasing and large areas of the foothills are covered in orange and lemon groves. Tuna, cod and sardine fishing and canning are important, but the industry has not modernised and faces strong competition from Spanish fishermen with more modern fleets.

Natural sculptures formed from the rock at Algar Seco

Essence of the Algarve

Landscape and climate combine in the Algarve to create a region of year-round appeal. In winter the Algarve basks in balmy sunshine. In summer it remains green and equable due to the cooling effect of Atlantic breezes. Travelling around, you will encounter breathtaking views: sheer cliffs battered by Atlantic waves at Cabo de São Vicente (Cape St Vincent); sheltered valleys with their patchwork of orange groves; vineyards and ancient olive trees or castle-topped peaks, with Moorish-style houses tumbling down the hillside; and gaily painted sardine boats in the harbours.

Nothing beats the taste of fresh sardines grilled on a wood fire

THE **10** ESSENTIALS

If you only have a short time to visit the Algarve, or would like to get a really complete picture of the region, here are the essentials:

- **Blow the cobwebs away** on top of the cliffs at Fim do Mundo (Land's End), as Cape St Vincent is known, gazing out over the rolling waves to the distant horizon.
- **Step back in time** on a visit to Silves, which under Moorish rule boasted marble-clad palaces and bazaars full of eastern splendour.
- **Go for dinner** in a traditional Portuguese restaurant and listen to the plaintive sound of Portuguese *fado* music (➤ 112).
- **Eat lunch in Portimão**, where fresh sardines are unloaded from fishing boats and cooked at rough-and-ready harbourside stalls, advertising their presence with the delicious scent of charcoal-grilled fish.

- **Walk to the Fonte de Benémola** (➤ 73) for a taste of the Algarvian countryside, as a contrast to the more developed coast.
- **Visit Praia da Rocha** (➤ 53) at sunset to enjoy the changing colours of the sandstone rocks and cliffs as the sun goes down.
- **Drive along the Guadiana River** and take a day trip to Spain by ferry from Vila Real de Santo António, to savour the many differences between Portugal and Spain.
- **Join in a village festivity** for the fun of noisy fireworks and to taste local wines and kebabs or fish cooked over an open wood fire.
- **Spend a lazy day** on the beach but, rather than joining the hordes at Albufeira or

Orange groves scent the air with heady blossom and fruit

Monte Gordo, head for one of the barrier islands, such as the Ilha da Tavira, and find your own private area of sand dunes and sea.
- **Visit the capital,** Faro, for its sophistication, its timeless Old Town, the ethnographic museum illustrating a way of life that only just survives, and to enjoy the *frisson* of the skull-lined Capela dos Ossos in the Carmo church.

Mesmerising waves beat against the Algarvian shore

The Shaping of the Algarve

2000 BC
Bronze Age people migrate to the region from North Africa and establish settlements at Lagos, Tavira and Lagoa.

1000 BC
Phoenician traders from the eastern Mediterranean establish trading posts along the Algarve coast, exporting salt-preserved sardines and tuna.

550 BC
The Carthaginians, from modern-day Tunisia, found the town of Portimão, known in the 3rd century BC as Portus Hanibalis, after the great Carthaginian general.

197 BC
The Romans invade the Iberian Peninsula and settle the Algarve. Resistance to the Romans leads to years of guerilla warfare until Caesar finally quells the

region in his campaigns of 61–45 BC.

5th century AD
Christianised Visigoths migrate into the Algarve from the north and settle in the region, establishing the first cathedral at Faro.

AD 711
Arabs invade the Algarve from Ceuta in Northern Africa and conquer the region over three years.

The caravel was a mainstay of Portuguese exploration

AD 712
Moorish leader Muce-Ben-Noçair adopts Silves as the regional capital. The Moors name their new territory Al-Gharb, the 'land of the west', from which the modern name for the region – Algarve – is derived.

1189
The Christian reconquest of the Iberian Peninsula achieves a notable victory at Silves, when the besieged city surrenders to an army led by King Sancho I, which is augmented by Christian Crusaders from northern Europe.

1191
The Moors recapture the city and continue to rule in the Algarve, long after they are driven out of Lisbon and the north of Portugal.

1249
Sancho's successors, Afonso II and III, continue the struggle against the Moors, taking Tavira in 1239, then Faro, and finally Silves. The Moors finally leave the region, which becomes part of the Kingdom of Portugal.

1443
Prince Henry the Navigator sets up his court at Sagres and establishes a school of navigation, ship-building and astronomy. As the sponsor of many expeditions to explore the West African coast and the islands of the Madeiran archipelago, he lays down the foundation for Portugal's subsequent pre-eminence as a maritime trading nation.

1444
One of Europe's first-ever slave markets is established at Lagos, following western exploration of what is now the Senegal estuary.

1485
Portugal becomes a major commercial power,

Philip II of Spain conquered Portugal in 1580

with trading posts in western and southern Africa, Asia, Indonesia and Brazil, but Lisbon takes over from the Algarvian ports as the departure point for voyages of discovery, and the Algarve becomes a relative backwater.

1580
The Algarve comes under Spanish rule after Philip II conquers Portugal.

1640
Border towns on the Guadiana River bear the brunt of the fighting as the Portuguese revolt against Spanish rule and regain their independence under King João IV.

1755
A series of earthquakes destroys many towns in the Algarve, and the subsequent tidal waves block river estuaries and ports with sand. The Marquês de Pombal,

King José I's chief minister, rebuilds the region's towns.

1807
Napoleon invades Portugal and the royal family flees to Brazil. The Algarve puts up fierce resistance to the French, and a group of fishermen from Olhão later sail to Rio de Janeiro in a tiny boat to tell their exiled king of Napoleon's defeat.

1889
The Faro to Lisbon railway is opened.

1933
President Salazar establishes a military dictatorship in Portugal. Portugal remains neutral during World War II, but severs relations with Nazi Germany.

1974
The Carnation Revolution: Portugal becomes a democracy after soldiers overthrow the post-war dictatorship. Flowers in the barrels of their guns are a symbol of peace.

1986
Portugal becomes a member of the EU,

releasing development funds for the improvement of the region's infrastructure, including the main east–west motorway and the bridge linking Portugal and Spain across the Guadiana.

1996
After years of drought that have left the region's reservoirs dry, the Algarve experiences record rainfall.

1998
Plans are set up to create a long distance footpath – the Via Algarviana – for the millennium, taking in the most attractive parts of inland Algarve.

Salazar's dictatorial regime ended with a peaceful revolution

Peace & Quiet

Almonds, introduced by the Moors, bloom like snow in spring

Away from it All

The Algarve is at its most developed south of the IP1 motorway between Faro and Albufeira. Simply to drive away from this area is to escape quickly and easily from the bustle of modern life and discover the many faces of the Algarve. South of Faro is the extensive Reserva Natural da Ria Formosa (► 26), a series of salt-water lagoons and salt pans separated from the open sea by scores of sandy islands, some tiny, others stretching for several kilometres. The warm lagoon water supports many types of marine life. This in turn attracts flocks of wading birds, from shy flamingos to the storks that flap lazily over the roof-tops, building their nests on church towers, telegraph poles and ancient olive trees.

Further west, the marsh systems and river estuaries around Portimão, Lagos and Burgau are full of birds. You do not have to be a knowledgeable ornithologist to spot the ubiquitous flocks of cattle egrets, with their hunched shoulders, long probing beaks and pure white feathers, or to enjoy the hunting skill of the kestrels and sparrowhawks that skim the fields in search of prey.

Bird Migration

The Algarve is also an important staging post for migrating birds, which pass down through the Iberian Peninsula in October before making the final leg of their journey to Africa. Returning the same way in March and April, they ride the southwesterly winds from Africa, exploiting the fact that spring and summer come early here in order to feed on the insects that are already thick in the air before heading for nesting sites in northern Europe. Cape St Vincent, Europe's southwesterly tip, is the place to see birds streaming past the cliffs or using the updraughts to carry them inland – these range from large seabirds, such as gannets, skuas, petrels and shearwaters, to swallows, swifts, warblers, and colourful bee-eaters.

Inland Algarve

The hilly Algarvian interior is covered in a network of paths and mule tracks, which are perfect for exploring on foot. Large-scale walking maps are difficult to come by and generally out of date, but the Algarve Tourist Authority publishes a *Guide to Walks*, containing 20 short routes, and more ambitious walks are detailed in the excellent *Landscapes of Portugal*, by Brian and Eileen Anderson (Sunflower Guides).

Walkers head for the Algarve any time from late October onwards, but the best time to come is March to

Algarvian Trees
The carob tree is widely grown in the Algarve because its long, bean-like seeds are used as cattle fodder. You will often see it growing in groves, partnered by gnarled old olives and fig trees. Mimosas are commonly planted along road verges, their puffy yellow flowers scattering a delicious almond-like scent during the spring.

May, when the countryside is a mass of flowers and butterflies. A short walk in the hills will take you from orange groves, heady with the cloying scent of citrus blossom, to bare slopes dense with sticky-leaved cistus (rock rose), bearing big white flowers. Rarer flowers bloom in the undergrowth, including many kinds of orchid, as well as numerous bulbs, such as the petticoat-hoop narcissus. Every wayside is bright with the searing yellow of the Bermuda buttercup, which colonises every inch of uncultivated space, and the sound of cicadas in the undergrowth can reach a deafening pitch.

Walking
The Algarve Walkers Club is a group of English expatriates living in the Algarve who meet for weekly rambles.
☎ 082 449098 for further information.

Walkers set off towards the atalaia *(obelisk) at Luz*

The Algarve's Famous

Henry the Navigator founded Portugal's global empire

The Moorish Legacy
Though the former great names of the Algarve remain unsung in the West, Arab historians list a number of Algarvian scientists, poets, philosophers and astronomers, and it was due to contact between Moorish and European traders that Arabic numbers began to be used in the West, replacing the cumbersome Roman system. These learned scholars also introduced many innovations in the fields of arithmetic, astronomy, navigation, medicine, agriculture, law and ceramics.

Henry the Navigator
Prince Henry the Navigator (Dom Henrique O Navegador, 1394–1460) was the third son of João I of Portugal. Though he only ever made one sea journey, he nevertheless single-handedly set Portugal on the course that was to make her one of the great maritime powers of Europe. He did this by setting up a college at Sagres, symbolically choosing a point that looks out from the tip of Europe to what was then the vast unknown of the Atlantic. Gathering around him the best astronomers, naval engineers and navigators of his day, he funded their research and their voyages of discovery. The invention of the caravel, a small, light but extremely buoyant and manoeuvrable ship, eventually enabled explorers and merchants to reach India, the Far East and the Americas.

Gil Eanes
Theorising about the possibility of land beyond the horizon is one thing, but sailing into the unknown is a different matter, and Gil Eanes (c1400–88), a native of Lagos, was the brave navigator who took up the challenge. Sailing round the coast of West Africa in 1434, he led modern Europe's first-ever expedition around Cape Bojador, popularly believed to mark the end of the world, with only boiling monster-ridden seas beyond. Proving otherwise, Eanes mapped the coastal waters and encouraged others to follow in his wake.

Bartolomeu Dias
In 1487, Bartolomeu Dias (c1450–1500) set out from Portimão at the head of the first expedition since ancient Roman times to round the tip of southern Africa. The storm-battered tip, which he named Cape Torment because of its extraordinarily unpredictable currents, was more optimistically renamed the Cape of Good Hope on the instructions of King João II, who saw it as the route to the riches of the East. The Cape was to prove Dias' nemesis, for he died when his ship was wrecked sailing round it in 1500.

Top Ten

Above: *the Moorish
castle at Silves*
Right: *traditional
festive costume*

1
Algar Seco (Carvoeiro)

✚ 28C2

✉ About 1km east of Carvoeiro, signposted to the left from the centre of town

🍴 Small café (£) among the rocks; several others in Carvoeiro

✋ Free

↔ Carvoeiro (➤ 47)

Pitted pillars, grottoes and crystal-clear seas await you at Algar Seco

If you just want to laze around on a beach, Algar Seco is an excellent choice with its colourful cliffs and rock stacks.

There is a marked difference between the beaches of the sandy eastern *sotavento* (leeward) section of the Algarve and the rocky western, or *barlavento* (windward) section. Armação de Pêra, to the west of Albufeira, is the axis on which the Algarve is tilted and the point at which this decisive change takes place. West of here the land rises gradually until it reaches the high cliffs and boiling seas of Cape St Vincent; to the east, flatter coastal terrain gives way to endless strands of golden sand, gently dipping into a warm and shallow sea.

The cause of the tilt is the collision zone between the Eurasian and African continental plates, which lies only a short way south of the Algarvian coast. The African plate is moving northwestwards, pushing the European land mass slowly upwards. This explains why the junction between land and sea is more dramatic in the west, marked by steep sandstone cliffs, and why the coast is broken up into a series of rock-strewn coves.

The result is a series of wind-and-sea eroded rocks whose evocative shapes make this part of the coast unique, and nowhere else has these rock formations in such quantity or variety as Algar Seco. Here, children will love exploring the rock platforms and pillars, the arches, chambers and caves, the miniature gorges, clefts and pools that litter the shore. Snorkellers will find weed-encrusted rocks like miniature coral reefs below the waves. There is not much sand, but the other features compensate, including the colourful show of light and shade that begins as the sun sinks at dusk.

2
Alte

*Discover the many charms of this pretty hill village, built around a series of gushing springs (*fontes*).*

Alte sits on top of a hill in the limestone foothills known as the Barrocal (► 67). Winding roads climb to the village through a region dubbed the 'Garden of the Algarve', where fig trees and citrus groves surrounded by dry-stone walls alternate with almond orchards and stands of gnarled and ancient olive trees.

The focal point of the village is the parish church, one of the most interesting in the Algarve because of its wealth of 18th-century woodwork and its baroque *azulejos*. Rope mouldings (in the Manueline style) decorate the west door, the vaulting of the chancel and the arch of the so-called 'Chapel of the Landowner', with its coat of arms of the counts of Alte.

Painted and gilded woodwork surrounds the altar while angelic musicians and cherubs scamper among the vine and acanthus leaves.

From the church, cobbled lanes lead eastwards to a series of springs, where the water gushes out of pipes set in niches decorated with *azulejos* and plaques inscribed with verses by the local poet, Cândido Guerreiro (1871–1953) in praise of water. The water here betrays its volcanic origins with a sulphur smell, but it tastes fresh enough and many local people come here to fill huge containers, believing that ithe water prolongs their life and keeps them healthy.

About 200m upstream is another set of springs, the Fonte Grande, with picnic tables and a popular restaurant specialising in folklore evenings. Keen walkers can follow the footpath upstream for 3km, to the source of the River Alte in the foothills of the Serra do Caldeirão mountain range. Less keen hikers will find plenty of shops in the village specialising in local crafts, and cafés with terraces and fine views.

Brazilian gold provides the finery in this baroque church

✝ 29D2

✉ 20km north of Albufeira

⏱ Church: daily 8–1, 3–7

🍴 Snack bar (£) and restaurant (££) at the Fonte Grande; numerous cafés in and around the main square. The Alte Hotel (£££) (► 103)

♿ Free

↔ Loulé (► 68), Silves (► 44)

3
Cabo de São Vicente

✚ 28A2

✉ 6km west of Sagres

🍴 Snack bars and cafés (£) in Sagres; Fortaleza de Beliche restaurant (£££) on the road from Sagres to the Cape

♿ None

✋ Free

↔ Sagres (➤ 37)

Come at sunset on a clear day to get the most from a visit to the cliffs that were once believed to mark the end of the world.

Cabo de São Vicente is the most southwesterly point of the European mainland (not counting Madeira, the Canary Islands and the Azores). It really looks and feels like the end of the earth (which is why the Portuguese dubbed it 'Fim do Mundo' centuries ago). With its towering cliffs plunging 70m to the pounding surf, and its stiff westerly breezes, this is a place that stirs the imagination and works a strong magic over the many visitors who flock here.

The Romans, recognising the spiritual pull of the spot, built a temple to the presiding *numen* (deity). Nothing now remains of this, but there is a lighthouse whose beam can be seen up to 100km out to sea. Officially the lighthouse is open to visitors if the keeper is not otherwise engaged – in reality, it all depends on his mood. If you do get to look inside, you will see Europe's biggest lighthouse lantern, lit by a massive 3,000-watt bulb.

Your own memories and impressions will be dictated by the weather: stall-holders selling chunky handknitted sweaters in the car park are a reminder that it can be chilly here no matter how hot it is a few miles inland, and there can be fog, rain or howling gales. On the other hand, nothing enhances the pristine beauty of Cabo de São Vicente more than watching sea birds playing in the air above the crashing waves, or the sight of the rose-tinted sun sinking slowly into the ocean at dusk.

Beyond lies only the ocean – the view from Cabo de São Vicente

4
Caldas de Monchique

Visit this centuries-old spa town in the Monchique hills and sample the waters to prolong your life and heal your ailments.

28B2

20km north of Portimão

Restaurante Central (££)
☎ 082 912203

Bus service links Caldas de Monchique to Portimão

None

Free

Built for indulgence – the spas and casino of Caldas de Monchique

Caldas de Monchique is a charming little spa struggling to maintain its position long after has it ceased to be the fashionable resort of bourgeois Portuguese looking for an instant cure-all. These days people come as much to enjoy the typically Algarvian food in many of the local restaurants as to put themselves through the strict dietary regime normally involved in a spa cure.

As with many spas built at the crux of the 19th and 20th centuries, the buildings reflect the belief that good company and relaxation are just as important for the cure as water consumption – hence a casino was regarded as *de rigueur* and the hotels were built with grand public rooms for dancing and conversation. Today these buildings have the added charm that comes from the patina of age and neglect.

The Romans got here first. More than 2,000 years ago they built a spa on the site of the present sanatorium, calling it Mons Cicus, from which the spa, and the nearby market town of Monchique, derive their name. Today it is the picturesque appearance of the little spa that appeals, set amongst dense woodland on the edge of a mini ravine, with its pastel-painted houses in fanciful styles.

Footpaths thread through the woods and along the river, taking you to various springs where you can sample the water – pleasant enough to taste even if it is warm and smells sulphurous. If you prefer something stronger, there are shady cafés where you can sip coffee, or try the local speciality *medronho*, a fiery liqueur distilled from fermented arbutus berries.

5
Capela dos Ossos (Faro)

*Intimations of mortality may occupy your mind
as you contemplate the skull–encrusted Chapel
of the Bones.*

*Skulls and bones are
arranged as if in a
decorative frieze*

✝ 63B3

✉ Largo do Carmo, Faro

🕓 Mon–Sat 10–1, 3–6

🍴 Cafés in the
pedestrianised streets
at the centre of Faro,
such as Avenida D
Francisco Gomes

♿ Few

✋ Moderate

↔ Historic centre and
museums of Faro
(➤ 62)

The Chapel of the Bones is a must for children, who find
this ghoulish chapel enormous fun.

Unfortunately, the Carmelite monks who created the
chapel from the bones of their pre-deceased brothers
would be horrified at such disrespect: the Chapel of the
Bones belongs to a southern European tradition of
reminding onlookers of their mortality and shocking them
into a more sober and upright life. Perhaps the intended
memento mori effect (the inscription over the entrance
translates as 'Stop here and think of the fate that will befall
you') would have been better achieved by a less decorous
arrangement of skeletal remains. As it is, the chapel,
completed in 1816, is too neat and tidy to be macabre,
with legs and arm bones used to create a classical architectural arrangement of arches, capitals and pilasters.

It is worth taking some time to look at the church to
which the chapel is attached. The Igreja do Carmo was
built in 1719 and has an imposing baroque façade, flanked
by twin bell-towers – its ancient grandeur now somewhat
compromised by its setting amongst modern tower
blocks. Both the main altar and the side altars are
decorated in the typical Portuguese baroque style known
as *talha dourada*, with extravagantly carved and gilded
woodwork, featuring scores of cherubs playing amongst
acanthus leaf and vine foliage.

Historically, the church has played an important role, for
in 1808 it was here that the people of Faro met, under the
pretence of holding a normal religious service, to plot their
ultimately successful resistance to the Napoleonic
occupation of the town.

6
Castelo de Silves

*The Algarve's best-preserved castle symbolises the
splendour of Silves in its Moorish heyday.*

The streets of Silves were once packed with traders,
bazaars overflowed with exotic goods, and the gilded
domes of many minarets gleamed in the sun. The bustling
capital of 12th-century Moorish Algarve, known as Xelb, is
today a sleepy place with 12,000 inhabitants. Only the
castle indicates the town's former wealth and importance.

The castle was built to last and, despite bearing the
brunt of fighting during the Christian Reconquest of
Portugal in the 12th and 13th centuries, it remains substan-
tially intact. Following the rampart walk, you can take in
views over the roof-tops of the town to the River Arade,
once the site of a bustling harbour, and across countryside
planted with the orange, almond and carob trees which the
Moors introduced.

Excavations continue to uncover the castle's secrets:
recently exposed walls show the remains of earlier
Phoenician and Roman fortifications and vestiges of the
palace of the Moorish rulers. Near by, the domed cistern is
still used as a reservoir for the town's water supply. This
same cistern kept the castle's Moorish inhabitants alive for
six weeks during the 1189 Siege of Silves. When the
Moors finally surrendered, the Crusaders went on an orgy
of looting, confident that the Moors would soon be driven
from Iberian Peninsula. Their joy was shortlived: Moorish
forces from Seville returned to exact revenge, and it was
another 60 years before Afonso III finally brought the
Algarve back to Christianity.

28C2

Largo do Castelo, Silves

082 445624

Daily 9–7. Closed public
hols

Cafés (£) near castle
entrance and alongside
the cathedral, including
Café Inglês (£) (➤ 95)

Few

Moderate

Historic centre and
museums of Silves
(➤ 44)

*Bigger than the town it
protects – the Castle of
the Moors at Silves*

7
Estói

➕ 29E2

✉ Rua da Barroca, Estói

☎ 089 997282

🕐 Wed–Sat 9–12, 2–5.
Closed Sun, Mon, Tue
and public hols

🍴 Sol Algarvio (£) and
Ossonoba (£) opposite
the church

♿ Few

✋ Free

↔ Vila Romana de Milreu
(► 24)

*Decades of neglect have only added to the charm
and appeal of the palace garden in Estói.*

Behind high walls, in the little village of Estói, lies a lavish
rococo palace, built in the 18th century for the wealthy
Conde de Carvalhal, Viscount of Estói. The family wealth
declined, and the palace was acquired by the Faro city
council some years ago, the plan being to restore the
building for use as a conference centre. The building
remains empty and unused, but the fine, formal garden is
open to the public.

Entering through a tiny gate in the estate wall, just to
the north of the parish church, you may be lucky enough to
find yourself the only visitor to this secret garden, with its
long, palm-lined avenue and terraces. Designed to please
the senses, the walls of the garden are decorated with

azulejos depicting bucolic scenes of shepherds and shepherdesses, while naked youths frolic with dolphins in the fountains. Elsewhere, buxom goddesses drape themselves langorously around water-filled shells, against a tiled background of cranes and bullrushes. On the lower terrace, a stone-lined nymphaeum shelters a copy of Canova's famous statue *The Three Graces*.

Bullfrogs croak and flop lazily into the water of the garden's several ponds, and nobody seems to mind that the upper terrace, with its weed-filled courtyard and pink-walled palace, wears the air of decay and neglect – on the contrary, regular visitors would probably prefer the garden to be kept this way, as they have come to love the softened outlines of crumbling balustrades, the crooked steps and loose cobbles, and the ghostly atmosphere.

Nymphs at their ease (inset) in Estói's aristocratic gardens

8
Milreu

Exploring the extensive remains of the Roman villa at Milreu demonstrates how little life in the Algarve has changed.

Dancing dolphins grace Milreu's Roman pools, spas and baths

✚ 29E2

✉ On western outskirts of Estói, well signposted from main approach roads

☎ 089 991620

🕓 Tue–Sun 9:30–12:30; 2–6 (5 Oct–Apr). Closed Mon and public hols

🍽 Cafés (£) in front of parish church

♿ Few

✋ Moderate

↔ Palácio de Estói (➤ 22)

At Milreu, you will discover that wealthy Romans enjoyed houses that are not so different, in many respects, from today's luxurious holiday homes.

The villa was probably built by a 1st-century AD fish magnate – perhaps the owner of a fish-processing factory, where locally caught sardines, tuna and swordfish were dried and salted before being packed in barrels for export. This theory is based on the fact that the wonderful mosaics that decorate many of the rooms show fish leaping in and out of the frothy waves. These denizens of the deep adorn the walls and rooms on both sides of the villa – the bath house to the left (west), with its hot and cold pools and its hypocaust system for providing under-floor heating, and the living quarters, to the right (east). Separating the two is a large courtyard garden which was once surrounded by a shady pillared colonnade.

Another plausible theory is that this was not a private villa at all, but a spa and temple complex. The huge building that survives to roof height to the east of the site is interpreted as a nymphaeum, a shrine to the local water nymphs, which was converted for use as a church in the early Christian period, reusing the pools and piscinas as baptismal fonts. Visitors coming to worship at this shrine would have used the bath facilities, which are somewhat grand just for a private villa. The sheer number of stone cubicles in the apodyterium (changing room) alongside the bath complex would seem to support the theory that this was a public facility – unless the owner was in the habit of throwing lavish poolside parties!

9
Ponta da Piedade

Consider taking a trip by boat to explore the spectacular free-standing pillars, rock stacks and grottoes of this cove near Lagos.

For coastal scenery, the coves around Ponta da Piedade are hard to beat. The same geological processes and erosive forces that carved out the rock sculptures at Algar Seco (▶ 14) have been at work here too, creating a coastline of ochre and rust-red cliffs, stacks and arches, which resemble the ruins of some fantasy castle.

From the cliff-tops at Ponta da Piedade you can walk along a path to the various sea grottoes (▶ 33), but the going can be precarious. From the lighthouse at Ponta da Piedade, for example, there is a narrow bridge that gives access to the headland with the best views, but vertigo sufferers may find it a problem. There is also a set of steps descending the cliff face from the lighthouse down to a rock platform where local fishermen wait to take passengers on short coastal trips to see the cliffs between here and Praia da Luz. This is well worth doing, especially during the nesting season, when you may get a good close-up of cliff-nesting birds, such as the heron-like cattle egrets and little egrets.

Another option is to join one of the boat trips that depart regularly from Lagos, such as those operated by Bom Dia. Trips usually last from 10 until 2, or from 2:30 to 6, but full-day trips are available as well, allowing time for swimming, snorkelling and lunch on board ship.

✚ 28B2

✉ 2km south of Lagos

🍴 Many pavement cafés in centre of Lagos (£)

✋ Free

↔ Historic centre and museums of Lagos (▶ 34)

ℹ Bom Dia Actividades Marítimas, Marina de Lagos (☎ 082 764670); 9–6 in winter, 9–9 in summer, closed Jan and Feb. Cruises daily 10:30–4, with sunset cruises in summer departing 7:30PM

Looking down to turquoise waters between Ponta da Piedade's rock stacks

10
Reserva Natural
da Ria Formosa

Learn all about the wildlife of the Algarve's lagoons, and meet an unusual breed of poodle.

✠ 29E1

✉ 1km east of Olhão, signposted to the Parque Natural, and *campismo* (campsite)

🕒 Mon–Fri 9–12:30, 2–5. Closed Sat, Sun and public hols

🍴 Small café at the visitor centre; plenty of choice in Olhão (£–££)

✋ Free

⬌ Olhão (➤ 86)

Sea life flourishes in the sheltered lagoons of the Ria Formosa

The Ria Formosa Nature Reserve stretches for some 30km along the coast, from Ançao, west of Faro, to Manta Rota, near the Spanish border. It consists of scores of sandy islands, linked by shallow lagoons, salt marshes and water channels, which are home to birds, plants and insects. While the outer islands facing the Atlantic bear the brunt of oceanic wind and waves, these shallow lagoons are warm and sheltered, providing perfect spawning conditions for many fish, and an ideal feeding ground for birds.

The best place for getting acquainted with the complex ecology of the reserve is to visit the reserve office at Quinta do Marim, 1km east of Olhão. Displays provide information on conservation activities and wildlife, and maps can be obtained showing recommended walking routes. You can also enquire about visiting the kennels where the rare Portuguese water dog, the Cão de Água, is bred to save it from extinction. These endearing 'poodles', with big limbs and curly black hair, have web-like membranes between their paws which enable them to swim very effectively. Algarvian fishermen once trained the dogs to help them by diving and shepherding fish into their nets.

Two areas of the reserve are readily accessible by boat: ferries depart from the harbour in Olhão to the Ilha da Armona (daily at 8:30, 12 and 5, last boat back at 5:30), and to Farol, on the Ilha da Culatra (daily 11, 3 and 6:30, last boat back at 7:15). From these sand spits you can watch the bird life of the lagoons, or find your own private strip of unspoilt beach and sand dune for sunbathing.

What to See

Above: *enjoy a drink in Lagos*
Right: *a Salema fisherman mends his nets*

Aljezur's sugar-cube houses are built in the Moorish style

Western Algarve

To the people of 15th-century Portugal, the western shores of the Algarve represented the end of the civilised world – beyond lay only uncertainty. Today, and even in the finest weather, the wave-battered cliffs of Cabo de São Vicente (Cape St Vincent) can appear suitably apocalyptic, and the Costa Vicentina, that part of the Algarvian coast that faces west on to the full force of the Atlantic, has some of the finest surfing beaches in Europe.

The west, being furthest from Faro airport, and lacking the long sandy beaches of the east, remains the least developed part of coastal Algarve, and is the part that appeals most to visitors in search of tranquillity, wildlife and the opportunity to experience Portuguese culture relatively untouched by the trappings of mass tourism.

> '*Where the land ends and the sea begins.*'
>
> LUÍS DE CAMÕES,
> describing the Algarve in
> his epic narrative,
> *The Lusiads* (1572)

Portugal's Atlantic coast offers some of Europe's wildest waves

+ 28B2
🚉 Lagos railway station
☎ 082 762987, 1km to
the north of the town
centre
🚌 Bus terminus: Rossio de
São João ☎ 082
762944, with services to
and from Aljezur, Burgau,
Odeceixe, Portimão,
Sagres, Salema and Vila
do Bispo
🔁 Luz (► 36)
ℹ Largo Marquês de
Pombal ☎ 082 763031

Lagos

Lagos is an atmospheric town encircled by massive 16th-century walls that effectively shut out the 20th century, including the western Algarve's biggest concentration of hotel developments to the west of the town. Holidaymakers tire of the beach and drift into Lagos to discover a maze of cobbled streets, too narrow for cars to penetrate. Café owners have set up tables and chairs, tempting visitors to stop and sample their delicious coffee and cakes, in between exploring the town's churches, its museums, art galleries, antique shops and bustling market.

Lagos harbour saw the start of many voyages of discovery

Parking spaces are available along the Avenida dos Descobrimentos, the palm-lined road that runs alongside the River Bensafrim. Sheltered from the open sea, the river was adapted for use as a canal to provide access to the town's harbour. Sleek white yachts and battered fishing boats sit side by side in the modern harbour, and signs point the way to the offices of companies offering fishing trips and voyages to the caves and coves of Ponta da Piedade (► 25, 113).

The social hub of Lagos lies at Praça Gil Eanes, with a huge statue of Dom Sebastião at the centre of the square. This modern statue (1973), the work of sculptor João Cutileiro, portrays Prince Sebastian, who believed it was his mission to conquer North Africa and convert the Moors to Christianity. He gathered an army of 18,000 men and set sail from Lagos in 1578. When his ill-equipped army met a vastly superior force at Alcacer-Quibir, in Morocco, only 100 Portuguese survivors emerged from the battle to tell the tale.

From Lagos to Luz

Early evening is a good time for this walk, when you can enjoy the setting sun. Ambitious walkers can take the whole route from Lagos to Luz; alternatively you can take the bus one way and walk back – check the times of buses between Lagos and Luz at the tourist information centre in Lagos. A third option, which is ideal for walkers with children, is to take the much shorter route to Ponta da Piedade and back.

Start from the centre of Lagos by walking west along the Avenida dos Descobrimentos, past the Forte da Ponta da Bandeira (➤ 34). Following the main road uphill and out of the town, turn left at the sign to Praia de Dona Ana at the first set of traffic lights. If you have a car, start at Praia de Dona Ana, leaving the car in the car park on the cliff-tops above the beach.

Explore the beach at Praia de Dona Ana, where the rocks are like fossilised sponge, then climb back up and take the cliff-top path that leads south.

Goats and walkers have eroded a number of tracks at this point, but they all lead in the same direction. Continue southwards, keeping the sea on your left, until you reach Ponta da Piedade.

At Ponta da Piedade, you will find fishermen waiting to take visitors on short trips to the nearby grottoes.

From Ponta da Piedade, the path turns westward and follows the cliff-tops. Porto de Mós, with its beach and café, is reached after about 20 minutes. From here, a track continues westwards, levelling out on the cliff-tops, and continuing for some 50 minutes to Luz.

The most prominent feature in the landscape is the *atalaia* (obelisk) above Luz, which marks the highest point (109m) reached by the cliffs on this stretch of coast.

Distance
6km; 1.5km Praia Dona Ana to Ponta da Piedade

Time
2 hours (long walk), 30 minutes (short walk)

Start point
Tourist information centre, Largo Marquês de Pombal, in Lagos, or the Praia Dona Ana car park
✚ 28B2

End point
Luz
✚ 28B2

Lunch
The Dolphin
✉ Rua da Calheta 14A, Luz
☎ 082 789992

A typical rock formation at Praia de Dona Ana

What to See in Lagos

FORTE DA PONTA DA BANDEIRA ✪

This 17th-century moated fortress was built to defend the town and port. Reached by a bridge and impressive gatehouse, it contains a small maritime museum, documenting the place of Lagos in the Age of Discovery.

✉ Cais de Solaria
🕐 Tue–Sat 10–1, 2–6; Sun 10–1. Closed Mon and public hols
💵 Moderate

IGREJA DE SANTO ANTÓNIO ✪✪✪

St Antony's is one of the most lavishly decorated churches in the Algarve. Early 18th-century carved and gilded woodwork covers the entire east wall and frames wall-paintings, showing scenes from the Life of St Anthony. Study the carving closely and you will find miniature scenes from everyday life.

✉ Rua General Alberto da Silveira
🕐 Tue–Sun 9–12:30, 2–5:30. Closed Mon and public hols
💵 Free

MERCADO DOS ESCRAVOS (SLAVE MARKET) ✪✪

Though not much to look at, this covered arcade, below the Customs House on the eastern side of Praça da República, is of great historical importance, for it was here, in 1444, that modern Europe's first slave market was established. Despite this, Portugal was the first nation to abolish slavery, as part of the humanistic reforms of the Marquês de Pombal (► 88) in the 1750s.

✉ Praça da República
♿ Few
💵 Free

Above: *St Anthony's life, set in lavish frames of carved wood and gold*

MUSEU MUNICIPAL ✪✪

This museum is packed with curiosities – alongside German pre-war banknotes and embroidered vestments are baroque religious paintings and sculpted menhirs (marker stones) from the 5th millenium BC. There is also a bust of the Emperor Gallienus, from Milreu (► 24) and a selection of chimney pots, showing regional differences.

✉ Rua General Alberto da Silveira
☎ 082 762301
🕐 Tue–Sun 9:30–12:30, 2–5. Closed Mon and public hols
💵 Moderate

PONTA DA PIEDADE (► 25, TOP TEN)

What to See in Western Algarve

ALJEZUR ✪✪

Aljezur is the largest town on the scenic EN 120 road to Lisbon. High on the hill above Aljezur are the ruins of the massive, 10th-century Moorish castle, captured by Dom Paio Peres Correia in 1246. He is said to have charmed a beautiful Moorish maiden who opened the castle doors to him one moonlit night. Good beaches near by include Arrifana (10km southwest), and Amoreira/Monte Clérigo (8km northwest). Some 17km north, the pretty, pottery-producing village of Odeceixe stands beside the river that marks the boundary between the Algarve and the Alentejo.

+ 28B3
⊠ 30km northwest of Lagos
🍴 Café (£) in Largo 5 de Outubro
🚌 Irregular bus service from Lagos
↔ Monchique (➤ 50)
ℹ Estrada Nacional
☎ 082 998229

BURGAU ✪✪

Burgau stands on the southeastern edge of the Costa Vicentina Nature Park, which extends in a broad sweep north from here to Odeceixe. The park encompasses 80km of coastline, whose poor soils and windswept salt-laden air have prevented farming and left an untamed landscape in which wildlife thrives – especially birds of prey and wading birds. Burgau makes an excellent base for exploring this region, with a good choice of accommodation in the village.

+ 28B2
⊠ 12km west of Lagos
🍴 Ponta de Almadena (£); several more on the seafront at Burgau (£)
🚌 Bus from Lagos
↔ Lagos (➤ 32)

CABO DE SÃO VICENTE (➤ 18, TOP TEN)

CARRAPATEIRA ✪

Sleepy Carrapateira owes its popularity to its proximity to some of the west coast's best beaches. West of the town is the long beach at Bordeira, guarded by the ruins of a 17th-century fort. Here the thundering surf appeals to watersports enthusiasts, but the sea can be much calmer in summer. Neighbouring Amado has the so-called 'Pedra do Cavaleiro' ('Knight's Rock') to protect it. Heading inland, the valley to the east of Carrapateira is noted for its wild flowers, which are especially abundant in May and June.

Bringing home the catch at Burgau

+ 28A2
⊠ 35km northwest of Lagos
🍴 Small café (£) in main square
🚌 Bus from Lagos
↔ Lagos (➤ 32)

35

+ 28B2
⊠ 8km west of Lagos
🍴 Numerous cafés,
including the Dolphin (£)
on the beach; Fortaleza
da Luz (££)
🚌 Bus from Lagos
♿ Few
↔ Lagos (▶ 32)

LUZ ✪✪

Luz marks the westernmost point of tourist development in the Algarve, and is an excellent base for family holidays. The holiday village here has won praise and awards for sensitive development: the whitewashed villas, dripping with scarlet and purple bougainvillaea, echo the shapes and colours of the older houses that line the road to the picturesque beach, and blend harmoniously with the natural topography. The sheltered beach at Praia da Luz has rock pools to explore, and a number of artificial scoops cut from the rocks that have been claimed as ancient (pre-Roman) tanks for salting and curing fish. At the height of the main season there is a well-organised watersports school and sea-sport centre in the village (▶ 113) offering facilities and tuition for sailing, diving and windsurfing.

From the beach there are cliff-top paths to explore (▶ 33), including one to the east of the village, which climbs to the Miradouro da Atalaia. Here an obelisk marks 109m above sea level, and offers sweeping coastal views. At the other end of the village is a 17th-century fortress which has now been turned into a popular restaurant. Near by, the village church has a pre-earthquake Gothic chancel, decorated with elaborate, 18th-century gilded carving.

Luz, with its well-planned
mixture of old and new

SAGRES ✪✪✪

Sagres is Europe's most south-westerly community. Just 6km east of Cabo de São Vicente (► 18), it sits atop a rocky plateau, scoured by the same winds that send the sea crashing against the rocks of the nearby beaches. Even more bleak is the promontory south of the town where Prince Henry the Navigator established his school of seamanship in 1443.

The sailors who came to study here lived an almost monastic life as they prepared to sail to new worlds, having mastered astronomy, navigation and cartography. The walls of the small town that Henry had built on the cliff-tops still survive, offering superb views across the rocky promontory, as does the simple chapel, with its altar-piece depicting St Vincent holding a ship. Near by is a 15th-century Rosa dos Ventos (wind-rose) inscribed into the rock, 43m in diameter, which may once have been fitted with a weather vane to indicate the wind direction. Other barrack-like buildings within the fortress walls contain a small exhibition on Henry the Navigator (open at erratic hours). The Vila do Infante, where Prince Henry lived, along with many other original buildings, was destroyed by the English buccaneer Sir Francis Drake in 1587, when Portugal was under Spanish rule.

Bracing as it is, there are many compensations to living in Sagres, including pristine coves to explore. Local fishermen keep the village restaurants well supplied with fresh fish and seafood, and also offer boat trips to view the magnificent Costa Vicentina from the sea. There are many cliff-top walks, and in spring and autumn you can watch migrating birds flying over the headland or wheeling

---

✚ 28A1
✉ 32km west of Lagos
🍴 Numerous cafés (£) around main square; Fortaleza do Beliche, (££) on road from Sagres to Cabo de São Vicente
🚌 Bus from Lagos
♿ Few
ℹ Rua 25 de Abril
☎ 082 442255
↔ Lagos (► 32)

Above: *a cannon at the restored fortress of Sagres*

Below: *pointing to all corners of the globe – the wind-rose at Sagres*

In the Know

If you only have a short time to visit the Algarve, or would like to get a real flavour of the region, here are some ideas:

Look for bunting strung across village streets – a sign there will be a festival at the weekend.

Discover the secret of eternal youth by drinking fresh spring water at any of the Algarve's spas, such as Caldas de Monchique or Alte.

Find your own desert island, or at least your own private stretch of beach, by taking a ferry from Olhão to one of the barrier islands in the Ria Formosa lagoon (➤ 26).

10
Good Places to Have Lunch

Fortaleza da Luz (££), Luz (➤ 93)

Mediterraneo (£), Lagos (➤ 93)

O Pescador (££) ✉ Rua Comandante Matoso, Baleeira, near Sagres ☎ 082 624192. Enjoy some of the freshest and best seafood in the western Algarve – try *cataplana*, seafood rice or grilled swordfish.

Florestal (££), Barão de São João (➤ 92)

Burgau Beach Bar (£), Burgau (➤ 92)

Paraíso da Montanha (£), Monchique (➤ 94)

O Cantinho (£), Portimão (➤ 95)

Café Alianca (£), Praça Francisco Gomes 6, Faro ☎ 089 801621. Forgive the slow service – the décor and ambience is the reason for being here, in

10
Ways to Be a Local

Hot and spicy chicken piri piri, *influenced by North African cuisine*

Visit a café and order a *bica* (strong black espresso coffee) for breakfast accompanied by sweet pastries.

Greet shopkeepers and café proprietors with a cheery *bom dia, boa tarde* or *boa noite* (good morning, afternoon and evening) as you enter and leave.

Buy lunch in one of the covered markets or shop early for tasty, freshly baked bread and the best choice of fruit, flowers and fish.

Join the fishermen on the beach at Monte Gordo or Salema, and watch them sorting out their day's catch.

Stay up late talking to friends over a drink in a seafront café.

Catch up on lost sleep by taking a long siesta after lunch, waking up in time to join friends for an early evening stroll around town.

Listen to *fado* in any of the bars and hotels that specialise in this unique Portuguese form of music (➤ 112).

Cafés are a second home, the centre of Algarvian social life

the dimly lit, wood-panelled interior of one of Portugal's oldest cafés.
Imperial (£££), Tavira (➤ 99)
O Soeiro (££), Alcoutim (➤ 98)

10
Activities

Walking: from forests to cliff-tops, from mountains to riverbanks, the Algarve is ideal walking country – buy the Sunflower walking guide for ideas (➤ 12).

Hunting for wild flowers: you cannot visit the Algarve in spring or early summer without being impressed by nature's profusion; buy a guide to the local flora.

Birdwatching: the Algarve's wetland marshes and lagoons attract wading birds big and small, from shy flamingos and stilts to storks, herons and egrets.

Keeping fit: make the most of the Algarve's sports facilities to tone up your muscles, improve your golf handicap or perfect your tennis.

Golf: the Algarve is renowned for its scenic courses; why not sign up for a few sessions with the resident pro.

Horse riding: beginners and children are welcome at any of the Algarve's growing number of stables, for a scenic forest or coastal ride.

Shopping for souvenirs: head for Loulé (➤ 104) for a good selection of crafts, or browse the pottery workshops of Porches (➤ 106) for a colourful hand-painted plate.

Sailing: with its many private coves and marine grottoes, the western Algarve is an ideal place to enjoy a short coastal voyage.

Watersports: learn to dive or windsurf with one of the several licensed diving and watersports schools.

Fishing: join a deep-sea fishing expedition and pit your wits against such game fish as swordfish, marlin and shark.

5
Top Souvenir Ideas

• Almond fruits – delicious almond paste sculpted to look like apples, pears or strawberries.
• A *cataplana* cooking pot so that you can re-create typical Portuguese fish stews at home.
• A large decorative bowl painted with flowers or fruits.
• Leather sandals, shoes or bags at bargain prices.
• A lace tablecloth or shawl bought in a street market.

5
Good Viewpoints

• Aljezur castle (➤ 35)
• Cabo de São Vicente (➤ 18)
• The peak of Fóia mountain (➤ 50)
• Silves castle (➤ 21)
• Alcoutim castle (➤ 80)

Decorative pottery

28A2
15km west of Lagos
Several cafés and bars (£) in Rua dos Pescadores
Bus from Lagos
Few
Lagos (➤ 32)

Salema's fishermen offer coastal tours to view the bird life

28A2
22km west of Lagos
Cafés (£) around Praça da República
Bus from Lagos
Few
Lagos (➤ 32)

SALEMA ✪✪

Despite the shops, bars and restaurants catering for visitors, Salema still has the air of an unspoiled coastal village, where the fishermen haul in their catch by the first light of dawn. Several offer fishing excursions to visitors, supplying tackle, tuition for beginners and lunch. Equally popular are birdwatching excursions, into the marshes west of the village. For sun worshippers, there is a sheltered beach at Ponta de Almadena, and another at neighbouring Boca do Rio; the two are linked by a 2km cliff-top walk.

VILA DO BISPO ✪

Vila do Bispo (Bishop's Town) was renamed after this former royal town was given to the Bishop of Algarve by King Manuel I in 1515. It was a rich prize, for the bishop enjoyed the revenues from the town's many windmills. Today only a couple of white windmills remain, minus their sails, and the structure that now dominates the horizon is a massive water-tower. Near by is the looming bulk of the 18th-century parish church, Nossa Senhara da Conceição, decorated with *azulejos* depicting dolphins, and dating from 1726. It also has a fine painted roof, and the sacristy serves as a small museum, displaying 16th-century painted panels and statues of saints.

Nearby Raposeira, 1km to the east, has a house that claims to be a former residence of Henry the Navigator. From the same period are the Manueline doorways of the parish church, its pyramid-roofed bell-tower and the chancel arch. Even older is the Chapel of Nossa Senhora de Guadalupe, to the north of the EN 125, east of Figueira, which dates from the 13th century and may have been built for the crusading Knights Templar.

Western Highlights

This drive takes half a day, but is easily extended to a whole day with lunch, sightseeing and beach exploration. The scenery varies from fishing ports and wave-battered cliffs to green river valleys and dune-backed beaches.

Head northwest on the EN 120, over the Serra de Espinhaço de Cão foothills, to Aljezur.

Climb to the Aljezur castle (▶ 35) and then cool off on the wonderful beach at Arrifana, where you can explore the ruins of an old coastal fort and look out to the Pedra da Agulha (Needle Rock) at the end of the cliffs.

Head south on the EN 268 via Carrapateira (▶ 35) and Vila do Bispo (▶ opposite).

Along this road, numerous unmetalled tracks lead down to the west coast beaches of the Costa Vicentina Nature Park. If you only have time for one beach, try Praia do Castalejo, signposted to the right just before Vila do Bispo. At the end of the 5km track it is a short scramble down to the cliff-backed beach.

Continue on the EN 268 southwards to Sagres.

From here you can visit Cabo de São Vicente and the lighthouse (▶ 18), or Ponta de Sagres (▶ 37), to see the site of Henry the Navigator's school of seamanship. Sagres is a good place for lunch.

Return to Vila do Bispo, and take the EN 125 east, towards Lagos.

Stop at Vila do Bispo for its church and the Nossa Senhora de Guadalupe chapel, beyond Raposeira.

About 3km beyond Raposeira, turn right to follow roads (some of them unmetalled but well maintained) through Figueira, Salema, Burgau and Luz.

Look out for birds as you go, and pick any of the beaches en route for a dip – or walk on the cliff paths above Luz. Alternatively, end the day at Praia de Dona Ana (▶ 33), watching the sunset from the cliff-tops.

Distance
120km

Time
6 hours

Start/end point
Lagos
✚ 28B2

Lunch
O Pescador (£££)
✉ Rua Comandante Matoso, Baleeira, south of Sagres
☎ 082 624192

On the western coast you will often have the beach to yourself

Western Central Algarve

Between Lagos in the west and Albufeira in the east, western central Algrave takes in a stretch of coast that combines attractive resorts with port towns, where catering to tourism takes second place to fishing and fish processing. Inland lies Porches, the centre of the Algarvian pottery industry, and Silves, a majestic hilltown with enough history to satisfy any culture-seeking visitor.

Beyond the fertile valleys around Silves lie the foothills of the Serra de Monchique. Here two huge reservoirs trap rainfall and spring water, supplying the region's drinking water and providing recreational facilities for anglers and boating enthusiasts. Northwards again are the pretty villages of the Monchique mountains, offering cool summer retreats from the baking-hot coast, and miles of tree-shaded footpaths, as well as the Algarve's highest peak, at Fóia (902m).

> *'Protected by a strong wall, [Silves] possesses a port and shipyard and is fine in appearance, with attractive buildings and well-furnished bazaars.'*
>
> IDRISI
> 12th-century Arab chronicler

Sculpted cliffs and coloured sands are the trademark of Praia da Rocha

The stones of Silves tell the story of the town's Moorish past

Silves

Silves is a compact town built on a series of terraces between the River Arade and the massive castle. One way to approach the town is by sailing upriver from Portimão (► 113 for details of river cruises) following the same route taken by Phoenician traders who established their base here in the 1st millennium BC. Their riverside colony grew to become the Roman city of Silbis, and then, from the 8th century, the Moorish city of Xelb. Described by Arabic chroniclers as 10 times more impressive than Lisbon, Xelb was a city of gleaming domes and minarets, of poets, writers and musicians, traders, craftsmen and farmers.

Due to the earthquake of 1755, little now survives of the Arabic influence – at least in architectural terms. The most lasting legacy is visible in the almond and citrus groves that you see as you look down from the castle walls (► 21) across the surrounding countryside. It was the Moors who introduced these crops, along with the irrigation system.

From the castle, narrow cobbled streets descend steeply to the cathedral and the archaeological museum. From the museum it is a short stroll through the Torreão das Portas da Cidade, the medieval town gate, to the main square, the Praça do Municipio, with its town hall, ancient pillory and pavement cafés. Shop-lined streets lead from here down to the covered market and the embankments of the River Arade, where pavement cafés offer freshly grilled fish for lunch and a view of the town's medieval bridge.

What to See in Silves

CASTELO (➤ 21, TOP TEN)

CRUZ DE PORTUGAL ✪
Sited beside a busy roundabout on the northeastern entrance to the city, the Cross of Portugal is a beautiful religious sculpture dating from the early 16th century. Depicted on one side is the Crucifixion; on the other a *pietà* (Mary grieving over the body of her crucified son). Such crosses were erected at key points along medieval pilgrim routes and this is a rare surviving example.

✉ 1km northeast of town, on the road to São Bartolomeu de Messines
🕐 Daily 9–6
♿ Few
💶 Free

MUSEU MUNICIPAL DE ARQUEOLOGIA ✪✪
The archaeological museum is built around the excavated remains of a Moorish house. The complexity and beauty of the well, with its stone flagged spiral staircase lit by arched windows, descending to the watery depths, makes you realise how impressive the Moorish city must have been. Sadly there are only fragments of pottery to fill in the

picture, though the museum explains the city's evolution thoroughly, from prehistoric to recent times. The top floor contains temporary displays, and the doors lead out on to a restored section of the city wall, from where there is a view down over the old Moorish quarter.

✉ Rua das Portas de Loulé 14
☎ 082 444832
🕐 Daily 10–12:30, 2:30–6. Closed public hols
♿ Good
💶 Moderate

SÉ (CATHEDRAL) ✪✪✪
Built on the site of the Moorish mosque to symbolise the expulsion of the Moors from the city, the magnificent 13th- to 15th-century cathedral is one of only a few in the Algarve to retain its medieval feel. Free from the gilded baroque woodwork of many post-earth-quake churches, the rose-pink granite columns and vaults soar above the tombs of medieval knights and bishops. Outside, the top of the granite wall lining the steps up to the cathedral has been polished smooth by generations of children using it as a slide.

✉ Rua da Sé
🕐 Daily 8:30–6:30. Closed Mon and public hols
♿ Few
💶 Free

45

What to See in Western Central Algarve

ALGAR SECO (► 16, TOP TEN)

ALGOZ   ✪

Set amongst fig, orange and almond groves, Algoz is a typical agricultural village of modest, whitewashed houses, many with the decorated chimneys so typical of the Algarve. Two churches are worth visiting. The 18th-century parish church has a baptistery completely covered in 17th-century *azulejos*, and statues of the same date which are carried in procession during village festivals. High above the village, the Hermitage of Nossa Senhora do Pilar is decorated with 18th-century paintings of the Stations of the Cross, and offers panoramic views over the countryside.

➕ 28C2
✉ 9km northeast of Armação de Pêra
🍴 A Curva café (£), 25 Rua da Moinheta ☎ 082 574512
🚌 Bus from Armação de Pêra or Portimão
↔ Albufeira (► 66)

ALVOR   ✪✪

Alvor is situated on the eastern edge of the wide Baia de Lagos (Lagos Bay), a shallow, bird-filled lagoon formed by the estuary of four rivers. Fishing was the inspiration behind the carvings that decorate the portal of the 16th-century parish church. Local fishermen join the wading birds in the tidal estuary, searching for razor shells and clams, which are sold in the fish market on the harbour, and which form the principal ingredient of the seafood dishes served in local bars and restaurants. For a closer look at the lagoon, it is best to follow the raised footpath that winds between the salt pans close to the shore.

➕ 28B2
✉ 4km west of Portimão
🍴 Ababuja (£££)
🚌 Bus from Portimão
↔ Albufeira (► 66)

Fresh fish straight from the sea and grilled to perfection

Conservationists have long argued for the protection of Alvor from tourist development, but with only partial success: most of the hotels lie further south, at Praia de Alvor and neighbouring Praia dos Três Irmãos, both excellent bases for those who want peace and quiet, combined with the culture and shopping of nearby Lagos and Portimão.

Did you know?

King João II died in Alvor in 1495. Dropsy was given as the official cause of his death, but many suspected that he was poisoned by Spaniards, intent on the conquest of Portugal.

Vertical cliffs enclose a perfect cove at Senhora da Rocha

ARMAÇÃO DE PÊRA ✪

Armação de Pêra is a burgeoning resort full of multi-storey apartment blocks and hotels, sprawling along a broad stretch of sandy beach that marks the watershed between the rocky coves of the western Algarve and the sandy shores of the east. Visitors can laze on the sands within sight of the colourfully painted boats belonging to the local fishing fleet, or engage in the many activities on offer, such as surfing at Vale de Centianes, or snorkelling at Marinha or Albandeira.

Nearby Senhora da Rocha has adjacent bays sheltered by high cliffs and connected by a rock tunnel. Perched high on the cliff above is the delightful Ermida de Nossa Senhora da Rocha (Hermitage of Our Lady of the Rock) with its candle-lit interior and hexagonal spire (▶ 58).

CALDAS DE MONCHIQUE (▶ 19, TOP TEN)

CARVOEIRO ✪

Carvoeiro is a pretty fishing village which remained virtually untouched until the 1980s, when tourist development began to spread rapidly westwards. Ringed by Moorish-style buildings and the battlemented remains of former fortifications, the sheltered beach can get very crowded at the height of the season, but local fishermen will happily take visitors on trips to the other beaches, such as Benagil and Marinha, and to the nearby caves, tunnels and rock stacks of Algar Seco (▶ 16).

🔢 28C2
✉ 12km west of Albufeira
🍴 Cafés (£) and fish restaurants (£££) in Largo 25 de Abril and along the seafront
🚌 Buses from Portimão and Albufeira
↔ Albufeira (▶ 66)
ℹ Avenida Marginal ☎ 082 312145

🔢 28C2
✉ 16km east of Portimão
🍴 Cafés (£) and seafood restaurants (££) in Estrada do Farol
🚌 Buses from Portimão
↔ Portimão (▶ 52)
ℹ Praia do Carvoeiro ☎ 082 357728

🔲 28C2
✉ 4km east of Portimão
🍴 Cafés (£) around the main square
🚌 Buses from Portimão and Albufeira
🔁 Portimão (➤ 52)

ESTÔMBAR ⭐

Estômbar is a former salt-trading town, with a pretty church, Igreja di Sant'Iago, which is worth a stop for its ornate baroque façade. Typical of the 16th-century Manueline style, its portal is carved with nautical motifs, including stylised shells and ropes in stone. Inside, the columns of the same date are carved with scenes from everyday life. The 18th-century *azulejos* depict St James in combat with the Moors, and the Battle of Lepanto (1571), a famous victory for Christian forces against the might of the Ottoman Turkish navy, as well as more conventional religious scenes.

More appealing to children is the big Slide and Splash aquapark (➤ 110), east of town.

🔲 28C2
✉ 2km east of Portimão
🍴 Cafés (£) along the harbour front
🚌 Buses from Portimão and Albufeira
🔁 Portimão (➤ 52)

Unspoiled Ferragudo

FERRAGUDO ⭐⭐

Located on the opposite side of the Arade River estuary from Portimão, Ferragudo is a rare example of an almost untouched coastal fishing village, a reminder of the Algarve as it was less than two decades ago. A timeless atmosphere prevails in the narrow cobbled streets which lead uphill to the simple village church, from whose terrace there are sweeping views over the roof-tops across the boat-filled estuary.

To the south of the village, the remains of the Castelo de São João de Arade stand on a rocky headland. This medieval fortress, along with the Forte de Santa Catarina on the opposite bank, was built to keep a watch for hostile ships and to prevent them penetrating too far up the river. Now a private house, the fort was turned into a romantic home by the poet Coelho Carvalho at the beginning of the 20th century. From the castle, it is a short stroll to the magnificent Praia Grande. This sandy beach, protected from the open sea by a *molhe* (sea wall), is a good place to learn windsurfing, while a short way further south, a light-house guides ships up to the main estuary channel.

GUIA ✪

Although Guia has an interesting church, richly decorated with *azulejo* tile pictures, the real attraction here is the Zoomarine Park (➤ 110) on the edge of this crossroads village. The park combines various attractions: a swimming pool, a pirate castle and a mini-fairground, with a big wheel, a bouncy castle and merry-go-rounds. There are performing dolphins, sealions and parrots, and various animals and marine creatures, including seals, sharks and penguins, are displayed in aquaria and enclosures around the park.

✚ 28C2
✉ 4km northwest of Albufeira
🍴 Cafés (£) around the main square
🚌 Buses from Albufeira
↔ Albufeira (➤ 66)

LAGOA ✪✪

Lagoa is the Algarve's main wine-producing town, and the local co-operative, on the Portimão road, offers guided tours and wine tastings. As well as making both light and full-bodied red wines, the co-operative also produces *aguardente*, a sugar-cane spirit, taken as an aperitif. Another local product worth looking out for is *morgadinhos* – almond-paste sweets in the shape of animals and flowers.

✚ 28C2
✉ 8km east of Portimão
🍴 Cafés (£) around the main square
🚌 Buses from Portimão and Albufeira
↔ Portimão (➤ 52)

Adega Co-operativa de Lagoa
✉ EN 125, Portimão road
☎ 082 342181 (book 24 hours in advance)
🕐 Daily 9:30–12:30, 2–5:30
🎟 Free

Though no longer the big event it once was, Holy Week is still marked in Lagoa with processions and prayers. The parish church has an 18th-century altar noted for its statue of Nossa Senhora da Luz (Our Lady of Light). Two blocks north, the São José Monastery has a pretty cloister whose garden contains a menhir perhaps dating back to 4000 BC.

Above: azulejo *panel at the monastery of São José*

49

Traditional irrigation methods inspired this Monchique fountain

MONCHIQUE   ✪✪✪

Monchique, the main town in the Serra da Monchique mountain range, attracts summer visitors seeking an escape from the roasting sun of the coastal resorts. Located 458m above sea level, the tree-shaded town feels several degrees cooler. Monchique has many natural springs, and the nearby spa village of Caldas de Monchique (➤ 19) is the source of the commercially bottled water sold all over the Algarve. Springs feed the fountain that adorns Monchique's main square, Largo dos Chorões. Cafés, craft shops and art galleries ring the square offering free tastings of *medronho*, produced by distilling the fermented fruits of the strawberry tree.

Handcrafted goods with a Moorish influence in Monchique's craft shops

Ornate 16th-century stone carvings decorate the parish church, Nossa Senhora da Conceição, and the gilded altar has many charming details, including angels holding up the sun and the moon. In one of the side chapels, look out for the *azulejos* depicting St Michael in combat with the devil, and the suffering souls in Purgatory.

Many visitors go on to enjoy lunch in one of several restaurants lining the Fóia road that specialise in chilli-flavoured chicken *piri-piri* (➤ 94). You can work up an appetite first by walking to Fóia, the Algarve's highest peak (➤ 59), or following the signposted footpath above the town hall that leads to the ruins of Nossa Senhora do Desterro monastery, a short stroll with fine views.

From Monchique to Caldas de Monchique

This gentle stroll takes you through the attractively wooded countryside surrounding Monchique to the pretty spa town of Caldas de Monchique (► 19).

Start in Monchique's main square, Largo dos Chorões. Head south on the main EN 266 Portimão road.

During spring, you will enjoy the almond-like scent from the mimosa trees that line many of the roads around Monchique.

After 10 minutes, you will reach the junction between the main Portimão road and the Alferce road, which goes off to the left (east). There is a petrol station on the right. Take the track between the petrol station and the restaurant.

The wide track now follows the right bank of one of the many small streams that spring up in the Serra da Monchique, eventually flowing down to the sea at Portimão. The track descends through olive groves and orange plantations. To the left you may catch sight of Picota, the Algarve's second highest peak (774m).

After 25 minutes or so, you will cross the Marmelete road. Cross to the continuation of the track on the opposite side of the road. Where the track forks, after five minutes, stay on the main track, which bears left. Continue downhill to Caldas de Monchique – the track runs parallel to the main EN 266 road to Caldas de Monchique for most of its length.

As you approach Caldas, look out for the strawberry trees that grow abundantly in the humid environment of the spa town. The fruits of these low-growing evergreen trees are used to produce a fermented liquor which is distilled to make *medronho*. Reward yourself with a glass on completing the walk, but beware – the deceptively smooth taste disguises a 90 per cent proof alcoholic kick.

Distance
4km

Time
1½ hours

Start point
Tourist information centre, Largo dos Chorões, Monchique
✚ 28B3

End point
Caldas de Monchique
✚ 28B3

Lunch
Restaurante Central (££)
✉ Caldas de Monchique
☎ 082 912203

Almond-scented mimosas in bloom in Monchique's woods

✚ 28C2
✉ On the EN 125 highway, 16km east of Portimão
🍴 O Leão de Porches (££)
🚌 Buses from Portimão and Albufeira
🔄 Carvoeiro (► 47)

Below: every comfort is provided on this traditional tour boat

✚ 28B2
✉ 18km east of Lagos
🍴 Cafés and restaurants along the quayside
🚉 Railway station 1km to the northwest of the city centre, on Largo Ferra Prado
🚌 Bus station on Largo do Dique ☎ 082 418120. Buses to Albufeira, Alvor, Armação de Pêra, Faro, Ferragudo, Lagoa, Lagos, Loulé, Monchique, Praia da Rocha, Silves and Torralta
ℹ Largo 1 de Dezembro ☎ 082 419131

PORCHES   ✪✪

Porches is the centre of the Algarve's pottery industry. Though the village is small, there is plenty to see here, as you browse through the displays of terracotta jars and watch artists at work, painting plates and fruit bowls with sunflowers, cockerels or colourful clusters of grapes. Be sure to check whether flower pots and urns are frost proof, otherwise they will shatter if left out over the winter in northern European climes. A trip to Porches can be combined with a visit to The Big One theme park (► 110), between Porches and Alcantarilha.

PORTIMÃO   ✪✪✪

Portimão is one of the Algarve's main fishing ports, and there is much local life to be enjoyed in and around the city's harbour. The appetising scent of quayside restaurants invites people to come and enjoy a plate of freshly grilled sardines.

If sardines are too humble, you could always take up the challenge of catching your own supper – tuna, perhaps, or hammerhead shark. Fishing trips, for beginners and experienced anglers, are advertised around the quay (► 113). Other options include Arade River cruises to Silves, and trips to explore the caves and cliffs at Algar Seco (► 16).

Portimão, with its good selection of high-quality shops, is also an excellent place to visit if you prefer real shops to those geared to tourists. Heading inland from the harbour, Rua Dr João Vitorino, Largo 1 de Dezembro and Rua Direita, along with the lanes running north to the parish church, offer plenty of choice. Largo 1 de Dezembro is laid out as a park, with fountains and flower beds, and the bench backs are decorated with *azulejo* pictures depicting key events in Portuguese history. The pictures date from 1924, when Portimão was granted city status by the Portuguese president, Manuel Teixeira Gomes, a native of the town. The adjacent town hall is a fine 18th-century palace, once home to the viscounts of Bívar.

The 1920s were a prosperous time for Portimão and many of the buildings lining the city centre roads were given decorative tilework façades and pretty, wrought-iron balconies, reflecting the art nouveau designs that were then in vogue. One other building to savour is the Jesuit Igreja do Colegio, on Praça da República. This profusely decorated church is the Algarve's largest, paid for by Diogo Gonçalves, a Far Eastern merchant, who is buried inside.

Vast swathes of sand make Praia da Rocha an ever-popular resort

PRAIA DA ROCHA ✪✪✪

Praia da Rocha is one of the most photographed places in the Algarve, with its distinctive, ochre-coloured sandstone columns rising from a broad south-facing beach. This is also one of the Algarve's most hedonistic resorts, popular with young visitors dedicated to making the most of the nightlife on Avenida Tomás Cabreira, the disco- and bar-lined seafront road. At the eastern end of the 2km beach, the Fortaleza de Santa Catarina looks across to Ferragudo's Castelo de São João de Arade. The two fortresses form a 17th-century defensive system designed to guard the Arade River estuary. If you are seeking an escape from the crowds, take a boat trip to the rocky coves at Praia da Vau and Praia dos Três Irmãos.

➕ 28B2
✉ 2km south of Portimão
🍴 Churrasquiera (£), on Avenida Tomás Cabreira
🚌 Buses from Portimão
🚌 Carvoeiro (➤ 47)

Food & Drink

Algarvian cooking has absorbed Spanish, Moorish and African influences, but nothing epitomises the region better than the simple charcoal-grilled sardine, savoured out of doors at a seafront café on a balmy summer's evening.

Amêijoas na cataplana, a traditional seafood dish

Algarvian Dishes

The region's cuisine reflects the ready availability of all kinds of fresh fish, from eels, lampreys and swordfish to lobsters, whelks, limpets and barnacles. Lobster, sea bass, mullet and bream are costed according to their weight and seasonal price (*preço variavel*) – check before you order to prevent an unexpectedly expensive meal. Most fish are simply grilled over a charcoal brazier, to seal in the fresh flavours, but tuna is more often baked with a sauce of peppers and tomatoes, and stuffed with a mixture of sausage, bacon, tomatoes and rice.

Shellfish features in two of the region's most typical specialities: *amêijoas na cataplana* and *arroz de marisco*. The latter is the Algarvian version of paella, a rich, slightly liquid mixture of clams, prawns and fish, cooked with rice, onions, tomatoes and peppers. *Cataplana*, named after the copper vessel in which it is cooked, is a delicious stew of clams, sausage, ham, onions, garlic, chilli and herbs. The

Spanish-influenced arroz de marisco (spicy seafood rice)

tightly clamped *cataplana* seals all the flavour in, to be released in a cloud of fragrant steam when the dish is ceremonially opened at your table. Some restaurants offer up to a dozen different *cataplana* variations, using combinations of pork, chicken, lobster, monkfish, shellfish and prawns.

Portuguese Dishes

You will also find dishes from other parts of Portugal on the menu, including *caldeirada* (fish soup), based on stock made from the heads and bones of locally caught fish, enriched with paprika, onions, tomatoes and potatoes. *Bacalhau à brás* is fried salted cod with potatoes, onions, garlic, olives and eggs. The ubiquitous *caldo verde* (green soup) is a popular starter, made from potatoes, onions and finely shredded cabbage, with spicy *chouriço* sausage for added piquancy.

The perfect snack – cakes made from egg yolks and soft cheese

Inland Cuisine

Though fish is also popular inland, you will find dishes on rural restaurant menus that rarely feature on the coast. Pigs' trotters with beans and black pudding, or liver and rice, may not be to everyone's taste, but few can resist the spicy taste of chicken *piri-piri* (flavoured with chilli oil), a speciality of the Monchique region, or *caldeirada de cabrito*, a casserole of lamb or kid with onions, tomatoes and potatoes. Game (wild boar, quail, partridge and pheasant) features in season, and if nothing else appeals, try delicious *bife à Portuguesa* – grilled sirloin steak.

Wine

Although the Algarve has its own wines, they lack the finesse of nobler ones from the north of Portugal. Try white port (*porto branco*) served chilled as an aperitif, rather than post-prandial red. *Dão* and the similar *Barraida* are good all-purpose wines: both red and white versions are aged in barrels to acquire an oaky flavour, but the best remain soft and fruity. In hot weather, try something lighter – such as semi-sparkling *vinho verde* (green wine – so called due to its youthfulness rather than its colour), with a palate-cleansing lemon tang.

Fine port is a favourite after-dinner indulgence

➕ 28C2
✉ 21km north of Albufeira
🍴 Café (£) near the church
🚌 Buses from Silves
🔄 Silves (➤ 44)

Almonds feature in folklore and also in many sweet confections

SÃO BARTOLOMEU DE MESSINES ✪

São Bartolomeu is a typical inland town in the fertile foothills of the Serra do Caldeirão mountains, where almonds, carob, figs and pomegranates alternate with fields of wheat or vegetables. Rua Remexido is one of several streets lined by the characteristic Algarvian houses, with whitewashed walls and the door and window frames picked out in vibrant reds and blues. The street is named after the guerrilla leader who lived here for several years and who controlled much of the western Algarve in the 1830s, during the civil war between right-wing supporters of King Miguel I, and liberal supporters of his brother and predecessor, the late King Pedro IV.

The parish church, Igreja Matriz, is a fine building in a mixture of styles, with a baroque façade, an elegant stone pulpit carved from local granite, and chapels decorated with 17th-century tiles and 16th- to 18th-century statues.

Some 10km west of the town is the Barragem de Arade, a reservoir created by damming the River Arade, a popular resort for anglers, with watersports facilities and several cafés along its shores.

Did you know ?

Legend has it that the almonds which grow in such abundance in the western Algarve were introduced to the region by a Moorish emir whose homesick Scandinavian wife longed to see the snow. The trees flower between late December and the end of February, and the wilted blossoms resemble snow as they drift from the trees, stirred by the breezes of early spring.

Portimão to Monchique

This half-day drive takes in the historic town of Silves and the mountain scenery of the Serra de Monchique, but it can be extended to a whole day.

From Portimão, cross the River Arade using the old bridge and follow the minor road to Lagoa.

Church lovers will want to stop in Estômbar (➤ 48) for the Manueline portal and *azulejos*, and in Lagoa (➤ 49) for the São José Monastery, with its pretty cloister.

From Lagoa, head north on the EN 124 to Silves.

Approaching Silves from the south gives a fine view of the walled hilltown and its castle. Park by the river and climb up to the castle, cathedral and archaeological museum (➤ 44).

Leave Silves on the road to São Bartolomeu de Messines, stopping to look at the Cruz de Portugal beside the roundabout as you exit the town's suburbs. After 5km, divert left for a view of the Barragem de Arade reservoir. Follow the minor road that leads, via Amorosa, to São Bartolomeu, and join the IP 1 to Lisbon. Leave at the next exit, after 15km, signposted to São Marcos da Serra and Nave Redonda.

Many distractions along the route will tempt you to stop – you may want to take a closer look at the cork oak trees to see how the bark is stripped, or perhaps enjoy the wayside wild flowers.

At Nave Redonda, in the Alentejo, turn south to return to the Algarve along a scenic road that climbs to Monchique (➤ 50).

You can extend the tour by climbing to Fóia, the Algarve's highest peak (➤ 59) or choose a restaurant (➤ 94) and enjoy lunch with views.

Head south to Caldas de Monchique (➤ 19) and stroll around the flower-filled streets enjoying the fantasy architecture of the former casino and spa buildings. To return to Portimão, continue south on the EN 266.

Distance
110km

Time
6 hours

Start/end point
Portimão
✚ 28B2

Lunch
Paraíso da Montanha (££)
✉ Estrada da Fóia, Monchique
☎ 082 912150

Born in Lisbon, St Anthony is celebrated in many churches

🕂 28C3
✉ 22km north of Portimão
🍴 Cafés and restaurants in Monchique and on the Fóia road (➤ 94)
↔ Aljezur (➤ 35)

Rounded hills clothed in woods typify the Serra de Monchique

SERRA DE MONCHIQUE

The Serra de Monchique range forms a distinctive group of hills in the western Algarve. Running from west to east, the hills act as a barrier to cold air from the land mass to the north, helping to maintain the balmy warmth of the Algarvian winter. The woodlands are a mixture of cork oak, sweet chestnut and arbutus, with the addition of pine, eucalyptus, mimosa and great plane. The hills are volcanic in origin and the igneous rocks are quarried around the village of Nave, lying between Monchique (➤ 50) and the spa town of Caldas de Monchique (➤ 19).

From Nave, the EN 267 road cuts westward though the hills to Aljezur (➤ 35). Forest fires have scarred part of the route, but this delightful road passes mainly through leafy woodland, past hillsides cut into terraces for vegetable cultivation, and fast-flowing streams. On the way, Caseis is worth a stop for its medieval church and the nearby ruins of what is claimed to be a Roman fort.

🕂 28C2
✉ 4km west of Armação da Pêra
🍴 Café (£) at Cova Redonda, many more in Armação da Pêra
↔ Armação da Pêra (➤ 47)

VILA SENHORA DA ROCHA

The sparkling white chapel that stands on the cliff edge at Vila Senhora da Rocha dates from at least the 13th century – a worn capital in the triple-arched entrance porch is Visigothic in origin, dating back to the 6th century. The chapel has long been a place of pilgrimage for devout Portuguese who come here to pray to the Virgin in this idyllic spot. Below the chapel are the quiet beaches of Praia Nova and Praia Nossa Senhora da Rocha. Fishermen provide a casual ferry service from here to several other isolated beaches, at Albandeira, Barranquinho, Marinha and Benagil.

Scaling the Algarve's Highest Peak

This hike through the wooded hills west of Monchique takes you to the top of 902m Fóia, the highest peak in the Algarve. Begin early in the morning for the coolest walking conditions.

Distance
16km

Time
5 hours

Start/end point
Tourist information centre,
Largo dos Chorões,
Monchique
✚ 28B3

Lunch
Estalagem Abrigo da
Montanha (££)
✉ Estrada da Fóia
☎ 082 912131

Start in Monchique's main square, Largo dos Chorões. Take Rua Porto Funda (the top right-hand exit) and then turn left up to Rua do Castelo. Turn right to reach the EN 501 road, signposted to Barranco dos Pisões and Foz de Farelo. Follow the road for 1km, and take the track left, signposted Portela das Eiras. Climb up to the village on the broad track. At the crossroads in the village, turn right, then immediately left along a path that climbs through a cultivated valley, with the stream on your right. Bear right uphill, through eucalyptus woodland. After bending to the left and then left again, the path descends for a short distance, before climbing for the final ascent on a rocky path up to the summit.

Be guided by the cluster of TV masts that crowd the summit of Fóia. These will not spoil the fine views from the *miradouro* (viewpoint) on the mountain top, which stretch to the Atlantic in the west, the Barragem de Arade reservoir to the south and the rolling hills of the Alentejo to the north. There is a shop and café at the summit.

Impressive views from the lofty summit of Fóia

The easiest way back to Monchique is down the tarmac Estrada da Fóia road, the EN 265. Alternatively, look out for the track that heads almost due south from the miradouro, following a river valley to join the EN 265 road, cutting out a 2km loop in the road. Another option is to take the EN 265 road for 300m and then the track to the right that descends via Cruz da Fóia and Cascalho dos Erades back to Portela das Eiras.

Eastern Central Algarve

Between Albufeira (west) and Faro (east) lie most of the Algarve's big holiday resorts – Vilamoura, Quarteira, Vale do Lobo, Quinta do Lago and Albufeira itself – tempting visitors with their white-washed villas set around manicured lawns, and miles of sandy beaches stretching to the horizon. Yet, unless you are staying in one of these resorts, you need never know of their existence: most lie to the south of the main road system, built on poor sandy soils on the marshy fringes of the Algarvian coast. If the fishermen have seen their coast transformed, the rich and fertile inland region has scarcely been changed by tourism at all, and prosperous cities – including the Algarvian capital, Faro, and the second city, Loulé – offer the chance to flow with the mainstream of everyday Portuguese life.

> *'Five leagues to Faro thro a beautiful countryside. On the one hand the sea, on the other mountains. It is rich, yet not wholly cultivated. The occasional odour of orange gardens was like Mohammed's paradise.'*
>
> ROBERT SOUTHEY
> *Visiting the Algarve* (1801)

———————●———————

Colourful confusion – Albufeira's popular beach is also home to the local fishing fleet

Faro

🔝 29D1

🚉 Railway station is on
Avenida da República, at
the northern end

🚌 Bus terminus is in
Avenida da República, by
the port ☎ 089 589755,
with services to and from
Albufeira, Armação de
Pêra, Estói, Lagoa, Loulé,
Monte Gordo, Olhão,
Portimão, Quarteira, São
Brás de Alportel, Tavira,
Vilamoura, Vila Real de
Santo António

↔ Olhão (► 86)

ℹ Rua da Misericórdia 8–12
☎ 089 803604

*Ancient and modern
buildings ring Faro's
sheltered harbour*

Visitors arriving at Faro airport could be forgiven
for judging the Algarvian capital to be a dusty
industrial town with nothing to offer. So it looks
from the airport road, with its heavy traffic and
jumble of seemingly unplanned tower blocks and
light-industrial estates. Yet, at the centre of all this
chaos, there is a quiet walled city of immense
historic character, as well as a lively shopping
centre, where cosmopolitan Faroites meet for lunch
at the pavement cafés of the traffic-free streets, or
stroll after work in the cool of the evening.

The port is the best area from where to begin a tour of the
city. The 18th-century Alfândega (Customs House), with its
elegant wrought-iron balcony, is to the north of the port
basin, overlooking an obelisk commemorating Ferreira
d'Almeida (1847–1910), former naval minister and citizen of
Faro. From the adjacent Jardim Manuel Bivar public
gardens it is a short step to the impressive Arco da Vila
(Town Gate, with the tourist information centre alongside).
This imposing baroque archway, with its stork's nest and
statue of St Thomas Aquinas, Faro's patron saint, serves as
a stately entrance to the calm streets of the old walled city.

The 13th-century wall that protects the old city was solid
enough to survive the 1755 earthquake, but the handsome
stone palaces that line the streets, and the beautiful

convent buildings of the main square, all date from the latter end of the 18th century. There is a great contrast between the huge cathedral and the magnificent bishop's palace, and the more domestic streets to the south and east of the walled city, with their wrought-iron balconies and peeling façades draped with washing.

One or two of those nearest to the Arco do Repouso have been converted to chic shops and restaurants. Near by is a statue of King Afonso III, who in 1249 captured the city from the Moors and expelled them from the Algarve. He is said to have rested here after vanquishing the Moors, hence the name of the gate – the Arco do Repouso (Arch of Repose).

From the intimacy of the walled city, the arch leads out to the huge Largo de São Francisco, a square that is used for carnivals and feast days. Crossing the square, it is a short walk up Rua do Bocage and left into Rua de Portugal to the regional museum, and from there to Rua de Santo António, the shop- and café-lined pedestrian street that leads back to the harbour.

What to See in Faro

IGREJA DO CARMO (➤ 20, TOP TEN)

MUSEU ARQUEOLÓGICO   ✪✪✪

Faro's archaeological museum is housed in the Convento da Nossa Senhora da Assunção, whose elegant 16th-century, two-storey cloister survived the earthquake of 1755. The ground floor's archaeological collection includes Roman and medieval funerary monuments, Manueline window frames, a Moorish stele inscribed with Arabic characters, and finds from the Roman villa at Milreu (➤ 24). Upstairs the miscellaneous collection includes everything from dress uniforms and heavy Sino-Portuguese rosewood furniture, to art nouveau vases and kitsch ashtrays.

> ➕ 63B1
> ✉ Largo Dom Afonso III
> ☎ 089 824085
> 🕐 Mon–Fri 9–12, 2–5. Closed Sat, Sun and public hols
> ♿ Few
> 🍴 Moderate

MUSEU MARÍTIMO   ✪

Housed in the same building as the harbour authority, this museum contains model ships – from 15th-century caravels to modern naval gunships, as well as a collection of colourful shells and models explaining the techniques of the fishing industry. In contrast with today's high-tech factory ships, with sonar devices and sweep nets, the sardine and tuna boats shown here seem charmingly antiquated.

> ➕ 63A2
> ☎ 089 803601
> ✉ Capitania do Porto de Faro
> 🕐 Mon–Fri 9:15–12, 2–4:30. Closed Sat, Sun and public hols
> ♿ Few
> 🍴 Moderate

MUSEU REGIONAL DO ALGARVE   ✪✪

The grainy pictures and displays of saddlery, straw-weaving, salt-panning, net-weaving and lace-making in this museum give a picture of everyday life in the Algarve as it was until the mid 1970s, and still remains in the more remote rural regions. Among the museum's fascinating exhibits are reconstructions of typical village interiors and displays of ornamented chimneypots.

> ➕ 63B2
> ☎ 089 27610
> ✉ Rua do Pé da Cruz
> 🕐 Mon–Fri 9:30–12:30, 2:30–5:30. Closed Sat, Sun and public hols
> ♿ Few
> 🍴 Moderate

SÉ (CATHEDRAL)   ✪✪

Faro's cathedral is a fine example of both change and continuity, standing on the site of the main mosque of the Moorish city, which itself replaced the remains of a Visigothic church built on the ruins of the Roman basilica. The 1755 earthquake demolished much of the original 13th-century cathedral, leaving only the truncated stump of the tower. The interior can be deliciously cool on a hot summer day. The Gothic chapel on the south side, with its rib vaults and bosses, survives from the 15th century, and the rest is typically 18th century, with gorgeous gilded woodwork and blue *azulejos*.

> ➕ 63B1
> ✉ Largo da Sé
> 🕐 Mon–Fri 10–12, 2–5. Closed Sat, Sun and public hols
> ♿ Few
> 🍴 Moderate

Left: *calm cloisters house Faro's art collections*

What to See in Eastern Central Algarve

ALBUFEIRA ✪✪

Albufeira typifies the way that tourism has transformed the sleepy fishing towns of the Algarvian coast into today's bustling holiday resorts. Until the 1960s, only fishermen used the beach below the town. They still do, bringing in their daily catch every morning, but now they are surrounded by thousands of sun-bronzed bodies.

In the narrow, cobbled streets of the fishing village behind the beach, boutiques sell clothing and jewellery well beyond the means of local people, while the Strip, the road that leads from the beach to Montechoro, is lined by the bars, English-style pubs and discos that form the focal point of Albuferia's lively nightlife. The streets are attractively paved with black and white mosaics, a traditional form of paving that was originally invented as a way of using up the rubble from houses demolished by the 1755 earthquake. A good time to explore is in the early morning.

The beach nearest to the town centre, reached through a tunnel, is the most popular, but there are others near by. You can walk to Baleeira along the cliffs, passing the Xorino cave, where the Moors took refuge when Albufeira was reconquered by the Christians in the 13th century. At Praia de Galé, 8km to the west, the beaches offer windsurfing and scuba diving. Olhos de Água, 7km to the east, has freshwater springs welling from the sand at low tide.

Cobbled café-lined streets in the holiday paradise of Albufeira

ALMANCIL ✪✪✪

Almancil (Almansil) is a dusty town just off the busy EN 125, the Algarve's main east–west highway. Few would stop here were it not for the outstanding church of São Lourenço dos Matos (St Lawrence of the Woods) that stands right beside the busy road (on the northern side – slow down and look carefully for signs to the church from the main highway). The interior of this domed and white-washed church is entirely covered in blue and white *azulejos*, dating from 1730. The side walls have six scenes from the saint's life, including his martyrdom on a gridiron. The gilded altarpiece is typical of those found all over the Algarve and known as *talha dourada*. Just below the church, the **Centro Cultural São Lourenço** displays modern art and sculpture, and is the venue for regular concerts – mainly jazz and contemporary music.

✚ 29D2
✉ 13km northwest of Faro
🕐 Church open daily 9–1 and 2:30–6
🍴 Café (£) in Centro Cultural, or try Bentleys (££) on the Vale do Lobo road just south of Almancil
🔁 Vale do Lobo (▶ 74)

Centro Cultural São Lourenço
☎ 089 395475
🕐 Mon 2:30–6, Tue–Sat 10–1, 2:30–6. Closed Sun

ALTE (▶ 17, TOP TEN)

THE BARROCAL ✪✪

The Barrocal stretches from São Brás de Alportel in the east, across to Silves in the west, down to the EN 125 highway in the south and up to the Serra do Caldeirão hills in the north. Despite its stony appearance, this region is highly fertile, with deep, rich soils derived from eroded limestone. For centuries, local farmers have been clearing the boulders to create fields bounded by the massive dry-stone walls that are such a feature of the region. These walls, and the bare fields – known as *terra rossa* (red earth) – are rust red in colour, reflecting the large amounts of iron in the soil. Once cleared, the fields are ploughed and planted with oranges, almonds, figs, carobs (for animal fodder) and vines.

✚ 28C2/29D2
🍴 Cafés in Alte
🔁 Loulé (▶ 68)

The Barrocal is sparsely populated and villages are tranquil and unhurried. Wildlife flourishes; in spring or early summer, you will not have to look far to see bulbs and rare orchids in flower, and at night you will hear the sound of owls, bats and foxes.

Empty landscapes in the Barrocal provide a refuge for wildlife

To visit the Barrocal, take the road from Alte to Benafim Grande, then head south via Alto Fica, following signs for Loulé, or the road that runs further east, from Salir to Loulé and on to São Brás de Alportel.

🔢 29D2
✉ 12km northeast of Albufeira
🍴 Cafés (£) in the main street
🔄 Loulé (► below)

BOLIQUEIME ⭐

This once-sleepy village lost much of its tranquillity when it became a major traffic junction. The few visitors who stop here now do so because of the novels of Lídia Jorge, one of Portugal's best-known modern writers, born here in 1946. One of her most popular novels, *The Day of the Miracle* (1982), is set in a fictional Algarvian village called Vilamaninhos, loosely based on Boliqueime.

ESTÓI (► 22, TOP TEN)

LOULÉ ⭐⭐⭐

🔢 29D2
🚌 Bus terminus is in Rua Nossa Senhora de Fátima
☎ 089 416655, with services to and from Albufeira, Almancil, Alte, Armação de Pêra, Faro, Lagoa, Messines, Portimão and Quarteira
🔄 Alte (► 17)
ℹ Edifício do Castelo, Rua de Paio Peres Correia 17
☎ 089 463900

Loulé is a city to savour at leisure, arriving early in the day for the market and exploring the town's attractive streets and historic buildings before lunch. The second most populous city in the Algarve, it combines bustling modernity – symbolised by the space-age church prominently sited on the hilltop to the west of the city – with narrow, cobbled alleys where saddlers, metal workers and seamstresses carry on age-old craft traditions.

Parking can be a problem, but spaces are often available around Largo de São Francisco. From here, pedestrianised Rua de 5 Outubro leads to Largo Dr Bernardo Lopes, at the foot of Praça da República, the city's main street. The first right turn (Rua de Paio Peres Correia) takes you to the **Museu Municipal** (Municipal Museum) and tourist office, which are built against the few remaining walls of the town's medieval castle. The museum displays flint tools and pottery fragments from the many prehistoric grave sites in the area, as well as a number of Iron-Age stele (incised grave markers).

Opposite (on the corner with Rua Vice-Almirante Cândido dos Reis) is the delightful Espírito Santo

Space-age Nossa Senhora da Piedade on a hill above Loulé

monastery, with its quiet, shady cloister. Part of the monastery has been turned into a Municipal Art Gallery, with changing exhibitions by contemporary artists. Heading downhill from here, cobbled Rua das Bicas Velhas ('The Street of the Old Spouts') is named after the spring-fed drinking fountains, set below a coat of arms, at the bottom of the street.

To the right of here, Praça Dom Alfonso III takes you outside the ancient city walls for a view back up to the surviving medieval towers, then the modern Rua da Mouraria follows the line of the ancient walls for a short distance until you find the steep alley called Calçada dos Sapateiros (Shoemakers' Alley).

The narrow alley opens out into the square that is dominated by Loulé's Gothic parish church, **São Clemente**. The tower survives from the 12th century, originally built as the minaret, or prayer tower, of the city's Moorish mosque. Though now hung with bells, and given a short dome and steeple, the minaret is one of the few examples of Arabic architecture to survive in the Algarve. Inside are several splendid side chapels – notably the 16th-century São Brás chapel and the São Crispim chapel. To the west of the church is the palm-shaded Jardim dos Amuados, the enigmatically named 'Sulky People's Garden'. In the opposite direction, Rua Martim Farto leads to the Municipal Market, a vast

From mosque minaret to Christian belfry at São Clemente church

Moorish-style building that covers a whole block in the city centre. Both within the market and in the surrounding streets there are shops and stalls selling everything from animal feed and (sadly) caged songbirds to cheese, dried herbs, olives, honey and fruit.

From the colourful market, with its façade decorated with art-nouveau tiles, Praça da República runs downhill, back to Rua 5 de Outubro, lined with many cafés.

Museu Municipal
✉ Rua de Paio Peres Correia 17
☎ 089 415000 (ext 211)
🕐 Mon–Fri 9–12:30, 2–5:30. Closed Sat, Sun and public hols
♿ Few
🎟 Free

São Clemente
✉ Largo Batalão dos Sapadores do Caminho
🕐 Daily 10–1, 2–7
♿ Few
🎟 Free

MILREU (➤ 24, TOP TEN)

PADERNE ✪✪✪

Paderne is an attractive town on the western edge of the Barrocal. High-walled villas with beautiful gardens in the hills to the east of town indicate that this is a favourite retreat for wealthy Algarvians. For visitors, however, it is not the village that is of interest so much as the castle on its outskirts.

To reach the castle, drive through the village north-wards (downhill), and turn left at the right-angled bend at the bottom of the main street. As you exit the town, look for another left turn (signposted 'Fontes'). This becomes a rough track after a short distance, passing through cultivated fields. The track leads to a commercial water bottling plant, where spring water gushes from a series of spouts into a large, stone trough.

Turn left at the plant, and then immediately right and follow the red earth track that winds though fields. At the next junction, you can turn left and follow the track up to the castle, or turn right and continue until it ends by the river bank. Park and enjoy the view across the Ribeira de Quarteira to the newly restored water mill on the opposite bank. At this point a track leads straight on along the river bank. If you follow it for 1km, you will reach a pretty 16th-century packhorse bridge with its grinding stones lying among the weed covered walls. Beside the bridge, a steep path climbs up to the right and leads, after another 1km, to Paderne Castle.

There is a more direct route to the castle from the riverside car park – straight up the hill following any of the

✚ 29D2
✉ 12km north of Albufeira
🕐 Castle open 24 hours
🍴 Cafés (£) near the parish church
🚌 Loulé (➤ 68)

steep sheep tracks. The castle's external walls survive to a good height, including the entrance gatehouse, and the floor of the castle is littered with fragments of medieval pottery. Rubble fills the chapel that was built after the castle was conquered in 1249 in a fierce and bloody battle between the Moors and the Christian army of King Afonso III.

PENA

Pena, in the northern Barrocal, is the start for an interesting walk that climbs the cliff-like Rocha da Pena, a wall of limestone rising to a height of 479m to the north of the village. The walk follows a well-defined track signposted to the right of the Café das Grutas, then climbs through typical scrub, with a mixture of low-growing holy oak, cistus and dwarf fan-palm. A triangulation stone marks the summit, from where there are fine views, as well as ruined windmills to explore.

🜊 29D2
✉ 9km east of Alte, 17km northwest of Loulé
🍴 Café das Grutas (£)
↔ Alte (➤ 17)

QUARTEIRA

One of the first Algarvian resorts to be developed, Quarteira's utilitarian hotel blocks are a million miles away in spirit from the villas of later resorts, which mirror traditional Algarvian architecture in scale and colouring.

Despite its lack of charm, however, the town has a long sandy beach and a seafront promenade lined with seafood restaurants and bars.

In the old quarter, there is a lively fish and produce market, and the gypsy market, held on Wednesdays, is one of the best and biggest in the region. Just north of the resort is the big Atlantic Park pool and waterslide complex (➤ 110).

🜊 29D2
✉ 11km southwest of Loulé
🍴 Cafés (£) on Rua Abertura Mar; Sea Horse, Dutch Pancake House (£) on Avenida Infante de Sagres
🚌 Bus station on Avenida Sá Carneiro ☎ 089 389143 with services to and from Albufeira, Loulé and Vilamoura
↔ Loulé (➤ 68)

🔲 29D2
✉ 9km north of Loulé
🍴 Two restaurants (££) on the tiny square (➤ 97)
🔄 Loulé (➤ 68)

On Salir's ruined castle ramparts, only a few massive stone blocks remain

QUERENÇA ✪

A modest, but atmospheric, farming village in the Barrocal region, Querença is the perfect spot to enjoy a leisurely lunch, with two well-regarded restaurants on the main square. Choose between pavement tables with views of the pretty, onion-domed tower of the parish church, or interior views stretching for miles over the Barrocal countryside. As well as its carved and gilded baroque altar surrounds, the parish church has a small collection of painted wood statues dating from the 16th and 17th centuries.

🔲 29D2
✉ 14km north of Loulé
🍴 Cafés (£) on the main street
🔄 Loulé (➤ 68)

SALIR ✪

Salir's huge 12th-century castle survives in the form of a cobbled rampart walk, which passes some huge bastions of concreted rubble, all that remains after villagers robbed the walls of their facing masonry in the past. From the western stretch of the ramparts, there is a good view over the hillside olive groves and the patchwork of cultivated fields in the valley below to the Rocha da Pena, which marks the northern edge of the Barrocal region (➤ 67).

The castle is one of the few Moorish structures to survive in the Algarve, and its scale is illustrated by the number of more recent houses that now fill the interior. Though heavily defended, the castle fell to Christian forces in 1249, towards the end of the campaign to drive the Moors from Portugal. The parish church occupies a high platform (shared with a huge water tower) with fine views over the Barrocal countryside. Inside, there is an unusual *Last Judgement* scene on the north wall.

Fonte de Benémola

On this tour you will enjoy typical Barrocal vegetation, and get the chance to cool your feet in the pool at the end of the walk. Take a torch with you if you want to explore the nearby caves.

To reach the start of the walk, follow the EN 396 north out of Loulé, turn left after 9km (signposted Querença) but ignore the Querença turning at the next junction, continuing on the main road for 2km until the yellow Fonte de Benémola signpost on the right (if you go too far, you will reach a sharp left-hand bend that passes a mill and crosses a river; turn back and look for the sign on the left after 50m or so). The broad track to the spring passes between dry-stone walls, and there are red and white paint splashes on the wall to indicate the correct route every time the track divides. After 1km or so, cross a bridge and turn left.

It is another 1km or so to the first spring and there is an even more delightful spot 200m further up the track, with a rocky ford and a mossy pool. Wild flowers, along with butterflies and grasshoppers, thrive in the damp atmosphere of the reedy river margins and on the limestone screes around. On the escarpment above the springs are two caves, reached by continuing along the boulder strewn track, then turning right to climb uphill on a well-defined path.

At the next junction, take the right-hand track (not the one that continues uphill) and the caves are reached after 100m and 150m respectively.

It is impossible to penetrate the caves very far without a torch, but you can stand at the entrance and imagine what life might have been like as a prehistoric cave dweller.

Take the same route in reverse to return to the main road.

Distance
5km

Time
2 hours

Start/end point
Roadside car park, 2km west of Querença
✚ 28D2

Lunch
Restaurante de Querença ££
✉ Largo da Igreja, Querença
☎ 089 422540

Catching sight of bright butterflies is one of the tour's many pleasures

73

VALE DO LOBO ✪

🕀 29D1
✉ 12km south of Loulé
🍴 Several bars and restaurants (£–£££) in Rua da República; good restaurants (££–£££) on the road between Vale do Lobo and Almancil
🔁 Loulé (➤ 68)

Vale do Lobo ('Valley of the Wolves') is an attractive, luxurious holiday resort built among the dunes west of Faro and attractively landscaped with umbrella pines, lakes and manicured lawns. The developers have been careful to use traditional materials in the construction of the low-rise villas, with whitewashed walls and orange roof tiles.

The sandy beaches of Vale do Lobo and nearby Vale do Garrão (also known as Paradise Beach) are lined with bars and fish restaurants, and there are watersports facilities here and at neighbouring Quinto do Lago. A great part of Vale do Lobo's appeal, however, is its proximity to the some outstanding golf courses (➤ 115). There are plenty of organisations offering cycling, horse riding and walking trips into the adjacent Ria Formosa Nature Reserve (➤ 26).

VILAMOURA ✪

🕀 29D2
✉ 11km southwest of Loulé
🍴 Restaurants (£–£££) around the marina
🚌 Buses from Faro and Quarteira
🔁 Loulé (➤ 68)

Pastel-painted holiday homes line the seafront at Vilamoura

The purpose-built resort of Vilamoura has, as its focal point, a large, boat-filled marina ringed by shops, bars and restaurants. From here it is a short walk to the sandy beach, and there are further beaches near by at Falésia. The tall-masted sailing ship, the *Condor da Vilamoura*, takes passengers from the marina on coastal excursions, and the resort has excellent golf courses, tennis centres, fitness centres, horse-riding schools and watersports facilities, all within walking distance. Though the resort looks and feels very modern, there was a Roman town here, and a Moorish settlement. Immediately to the north of the marina, archaeologists have found the remains of a Roman villa with bath suite, and a later Moorish farm.

Central Highlights

This drive takes in farming hamlets, green river valleys, gnarled olive trees and scented orange groves. Consider stopping for a leisurely lunch in Alte or Querença.

From Loulé, head out west on the EN 270 road signposted to Boliqueime (➤ 68).

As you leave the town, a wide new road to the left leads up to the unusual modern church of Nossa Senhora da Piedade. It is worth driving up for the views from the terrace in front of the church and for the little 16th-century chapel alongside.

Continue to Boliqueime and take the road north to Paderne (➤ 70).

Wild woodland and olive groves give the Barrocal its distinctive feel

Take the road north out of the town and divert left to explore the well-preserved, 12th-century castle above the River Quarteira.

Drive on through the village of Purgatório, continue to Portela de Messines, then turn right for Alte.

Alte (➤ 17) is the Algarve's most attractive village. The church was built in the 13th century by the local overlord as a thank-offering for his safe return from the Crusades, and has some fine statuary and tile work. The river tumbles through the village, over a mini waterfall and past converted mill buildings. Continue eastwards, stopping to scale Rocha da Pena, if time allows, or to explore Salir castle (➤ 72).

From Salir take the minor road south to Vicentes, and turn left. After 2km, the road crosses a bridge, turns sharp left in front of a mill, and then sharp right. A short way on, on the right, is the start of the Fonte de Benémola walk (➤ 73). Continue on to Querença, then to the main road and turn right to return to Loulé.

Distance
74km

Time
7 hours

Start/end point
Loulé
✠ 29D2

Lunch
Alte Hotel ££
✉ Montino, Alte (signposted on the road to Santa Margerida, 1km northwest of the town)
☎ 089 68523

Eastern Algarve

Robert Southey's description of the Eastern Algarve (below) remains as accurate today as at the beginning of the 19th century. Away from the coast, the countryside consists of a great, rolling succession of hills, covered in wild Mediterranean scrub, interspersed with cork oak trees. Southey found it monotonous, but modern travellers will probably revel in the sight of so much unspoiled countryside. In the future, dense forests will make this landscape look very different.

The homogeneity of the central hilly region contrasts with the pleasing variety of the region's coastal and riverine scenery. The broad, flat valley of the River Guadiana, with its bird-filled shores and reed beds, is endlessly fascinating, and the town of Vila Real offers a gateway to the very different Spanish region of Andalucia. The coastal towns include the port of Olhão, the city of Tavira and the resort of Monte Gordo, with its glorious beach and holiday atmosphere.

> *'It is a strange country …*
> *mountain all round*
> *swelling, breasting,*
> *surging like a sea.'*

ROBERT SOUTHEY
Visiting the Algarve (1801)

Looking across the River Guadiana from Alcoutim to Spanish Sanlúcar

29E2

Railway station is on Rua da Liberdade

Bus terminus is in Rua dos Pelames ☎ 081 322546, with services to and from Cabanas, Cacela, Faro, Monte Gordo, Olhão, Pedras d'El Rei, Santa Luzia and Vila Real de Santo António

Olhão (➤ 86)

Rua da Galeria ☎ 081 322511

Wrought-iron railings mirror the elegant balconies of Tavira

Tavira

This distinctive town has a greater variety of architectural detail than most. Both banks of the River Gilão, which passes through the centre, are lined by noble houses with baroque window frames and balustraded parapets. Most have wrought-iron balconies, whose decoration is mirrored in the railings of the pedestrian bridge that links the two sides of the town. The hip-gabled roofs are highly distinctive, known as *tesouro* (treasure) roofs.

Wealth from the Portuguese colonies was lavished on Tavira's numerous churches, whose turrets and belfries add further interest to the skyline. The best place to view all this architectural diversity is from the walls of the castle (➤ opposite) on the south bank of the river. Cross the footbridge, take the first turn right, climbing uphill, past the tourist office, and pause to admire the superb Renaissance doorcase to the Church of Nossa Senhora da Misericórdia (Our Lady of Mercy). Above the portal, angels hold aside curtains to reveal the figure of the praying Virgin. Turning left takes you to the castle, and to the hilltop church of Santa Maria do Castelo (▶ below).

Heading north from the castle, turn down Rua Detraz dos Muros to Rua dos Pelames; this riverside street has some rare, 16th-century houses, distinguished by stone doorcases which survived the 1755 earthquake. Crossing the footbridge again takes you down Rua 5 de Outubro to São Paulo church (▶ below). Restaurants and bars line the square in front of the church (Praça Dr Padinha), and the streets running to the south and east. Look out for the latticed doors, made of turned and woven strips of wood.

What to See in Tavira

Beach huts offer shade and shelter on the Ilha de Tavira

CASTELO ✪✪
Tavira's Moorish castle was rebuilt after the Christian Reconquest, and the present walls date from the reign of King Dinis (1261–1325). From the rampart walk there are superb views over Tavira's ornate chimneys, roof-tops and church towers, and to the few short stretches of the town's medieval walls that survived the 1755 earthquake.

☒ Calçada de Paio Peres Correia
🕐 Daily 9–5:30
♿ Few
🎟 Free

IGREJA DE SANTA MARIA DO CASTELO ✪
Standing alongside the castle, Tavira's parish church incorporates the minaret of the town's Moorish mosque, remodelled to form the clock tower. Inside are the fine 13th-century tombs of seven knights of the crusading Order of St James, whose ambush and murder prompted the Christian reconquest of the city. In addition to the fine tilework and gilded altar surrounds, the sacristy has a small museum displaying vestments and chalices.

☒ Calçada de Paio Peres Correia
🕐 Daily 10–12:30, 2–6. Closed public hols
♿ Few
🎟 Free

IGREJA DE SÃO PAULO ✪
Entered through a classical portico, more like a Greek temple than a church, St Paul's is unusual for the heavy, dark woodwork of its two side altars, ornately carved but not covered in gold. The fine collection of religious statues includes a delicate 15th-century Flemish *Virgin*.

☒ Praça 5 de Outubro
🕐 Daily 10–12:30, 2–5. Closed public hols
♿ Few
🎟 Free

ILHA DE TAVIRA ✪✪
This 10km-long island, with its sandy beaches and sheltered bathing, is the most accessible of the barrier islands in the Ria Formosa Nature Reserve (▶ 26). Ferries make the short crossing from the Quatro Águas jetty, on the south bank of the River Gilão. You can also walk to the island across the footbridge from Santa Luzia, the seafront fishing village 3km west of Tavira.

☒ Just offshore from Tavira
🕐 Ferries run 8AM–11PM, May–Oct
🍴 Cafes (£) at northeastern tip of island
🎟 Free

What to See in Eastern Algarve

ALCOUTIM ✪✪✪

Alcoutim has the atmosphere of a timeless town. Life here moves at the pace of the horse-drawn ploughs that are still used to till the surrounding fields. Ferrymen frequent the O Soeiro café, just above the quay, and take passengers across the river to San Lúcar in Spain on request. There are no border controls, so it is easy to slip across the river.

Both towns are dominated by their castle. Sanlúcar's is the biggest – a massive structure crowning the cone-shaped hill above the town – but Alcoutim's is the oldest. The excavated remains of Roman structures have been overlain by 11th-century Moorish remains, in turn super-seded by a 1304 fortress. Both castles are a reminder of former hostilities between Spain and Portugal.

Besides Alcoutim's castle, the other good viewpoint in town is the Ermida de Nossa Senhora da Conceiço (Hermitage of Our Lady of Conception). This whitewashed church, approached via an 18th-century stone staircase, stands at the highest point in the village and allows intimate views down into the village gardens and across the flat roof-tops of the simple, cube-shaped houses.

BARRANCO DO VELHO ✪

In the empty hills of the Serra da Caldeirão, Barranco do Velho is one of the few settlements of any size, located at a crossroads in an elevated spot. Visitors come to refresh themselves at the cafés lining the main street before heading on towards Lisbon or south to the coast. The village is also popular with walkers and mountain bikers, who follow the broad woodland tracks that thread through the surrounding cork oak forests.

✚ 29F3
✉ 40km north of Vila Real de Santo António
🍴 O Soeiro café (£)
🔄 Castro Marim (➤ 82)
ℹ Praça da República
☎ 081 546179

Above: castle walls guard the border with Spain in Alcoutim

✚ 29D2
✉ 30km north of Faro
🍴 Several cafés (£) on the main street, including A Tia Bia (££) (➤ 98)
🔄 Cachopo (➤ 90)

CABANAS ✪✪

Cabanas is a fast-growing resort just to the east of Tavira. It has a broad, sandy beach facing a long sandbank, with a warm and shallow lagoon providing sheltered bathing conditions that attract families with children. Beachcombers come to look for shells and fishermen dig clams and razor shells from the tide-washed sands.

Strolling along the beach is the best way to approach the fortified village of Vila Nova de Cacela, a tiny hamlet consisting of a church and a few cottages surrounded by massive walls, perched on a cliff above the sandbar. The perfectly preserved fortress dates from the Peninsular War of 1808–14, when Napoleonic troops invaded Portugal.

➕ 29F2
✉ 5km east of Tavira
🍴 Café (£) in Vila Nova de Cacela
🚌 Buses from Tavira
🚆 Tavira (➤ 78)

CASTRO MARIM ✪✪✪

At Castro Marim there are two huge castles to explore, spreading across the two hills that rise above the salt flats either side of this fishing town.

The main **castle**, to the north of the town, was built in 1319 as the headquarters of the crusading Order of the Knights of Christ, founded in 1119 as the Knights Templar. The knights played a decisive role in the Christian Reconquest of Portugal. The older medieval castle is now entirely contained within the walls of its 17th-century successor, which is six times larger.

A rampart walk allows visitors to walk all the way round the castle, with views down to the fishermen's houses below, built with flat roofs for drying fish. Also within the castle walls are the offices of the Castro Marim Nature Reserve, from where walk leaflets are available.

The **São Sebastião fortress**, on the opposite hill, dates from the 17th century and is part of a much bigger complex of defensive walls that survive only in parts around the town. Like its medieval counterpart, the fortress served as a base from where to defend the entrance to the River Guadiana, bearing the brunt of hostilities between Portugal and Spain. Today, the two countries have abolished their common border and the modern suspension bridge, which crosses the river, carries the IP 1 motorway, 2km northeast of the town.

➕ 29F2
✉ 4km north of Vila Real de Santo António
🍴 Cafés (£) in Rua de São Sebastião
🚌 Buses from Vila Real de Santo António
ℹ Praça 1 de Maio ☎ 081 531232

Castelo and São Sebastiao fortress
🕐 Daily 9–5:30. Closed public hols
💷 Free

Castro Marim's walls, a formidable defence

The Salt Pans of Castro Marim

Salt pans backed by the bridge linking Spain and Portugal

The castle walls in Castro Marim look down on acres of salt pans, many of them in use since pre-Roman times. Now protected as a nature reserve, these salt pans, and the tidal creeks that run through them, are home to many species of bird. Take binoculars with you.

Begin the walk at the nature reserve car park, off to the right (easily missed) as you drive south on the road from Castro Marim to Vila Real de Santo António. Walking away from the main road, follow the raised path that threads through the reserve, with the main channel of the fish–filled creek to your left.

On your right, the flower-filled fields are planted with olive trees, where storks nest. These huge birds may flap lazily overhead from time to time. Also visible are egrets, dipping their beaks in the silt at the edge of the salt pans in search of food, and the occasional shy flamingo. If you tire of the heat (there are no trees and no shade on this walk) you can retrace your steps. Alternatively, you can follow the path all the way round the reserve. At its westernmost point it passes the still-working salt pans at Aroucas, where salt obtained by evaporation is piled up in a great pyramidal heap.

From here the path turns southwards, almost to the suburbs of Monte Gordo, visible (but not accessible) across the Carrasqueira estuary. The path follows the northern bank of the estuary, over several footbridges, before rejoining the outward path: turn to the right to return to the car park.

Distance
8km

Time
3 hours

Start/end point
Roadside car park, 2km south of Castro Marim on the western side of the road to Vila Real de Santo António
✚ 29F2

Lunch
Restaurante Pão Quente (£)
✉ Rua de São Bartolomeu Sul, Castro Marim
☎ 081 513033

COVA DOS MOUROS PARQUE MINEIRO ✪✪✪

The open-air Mining Park at Cova dos Mouros is well signposted as you drive south along the EN 506 road from Martim Longo, through Vaqueiros. Located in the empty, scrub-covered hills of the northern Algarve, this new museum has been created around the spoil tips and shafts of an abandoned copper mine that has been in use since pre-Roman times. Guided tours of the site take in tableaux showing reconstructions of Copper Age mining and smelting techniques. There is a ritual stone circle and a re-created circular hut, of a type still widely used in this part of the Algarve for hay storage. Display boards explain the history and wildlife of the site. In spring, visitors will see orchids and other wild flowers, while summer brings birds, butterflies and lizards to an area that has been designated an ecological park.

➕ 29E3
✉ 10km southeast of Martim Longo, 2km south of Vaqueiros
☎ 089 999229
🍴 Café on site
🕓 Summer Tue–Sun, 10–6, winter Tue–Sun, 10–5. Closed Mon
♿ Few
💰 Expensive
↔ Cachopo (➤ 90)

Mining heritage brought to life at Cova dos Mouros

29E2

✉ 7km west of Tavira

🍴 Cafés (£) in the main street in nearby Tavira

↔ Tavira (➤ 78)

Above: *earthquake survivor – Luz da Tavira's Manueline church*

Opposite: *Moncarapacho's unusual chapel and museum*

29E2

✉ Northeast of Tavira, bordered by the EN 125 road to the south and the EN 397 to the west

🍴 Nearest cafés (£) in Tavira

↔ Tavira (➤ 78)

LUZ DA TAVIRA ⭐⭐

Not to be confused with Luz in Western Algarve (➤ 36), Luz da Tavira has one of the few churches in the Algarve to survive the 1755 earthquake. Dating from the 16th century, it is dedicated to Nossa Senhora da Luz (Our Lady of Light), whose statue fills the niche above the large, imposing, Renaissance-style porch. To the side is another porch with the stone-rope mouldings typical of the Manueline style of the early 16th century, inspired by nautical themes. The altar surround is 16th century, as are the polychromatic *azulejos* on the steps and pavement.

The houses in Luz are worth a second glance: many have the distinctive traditional *platibanda* borders. Surrounding the doors and window frames, and sometimes running along the eaves and down the house corners, these ornate plasterwork bands are decorated with floral and geometrical motifs, often picked out in a colour that contrasts with that of the exterior walls. The chimneys are unusual, too: their filigree patterns reflect the art nouveau style popular at the beginning of the century, when many of these houses were built or modernised.

MATA NACIONAL DA CONCEIÇÃO ⭐

The Mata Nacional (National Forest) is located north and east of Tavira. Heading east from Tavira on the EN 125, you will see a sign on the left, just past the large Eurotel, about 3km beyond the bridge that crosses the Gilão River. In place of the expected trees, you will discover tiny hill villages, such as Eiras, approached by means of a ford – a good base for exploring a delightful rural landscape, similar to that of the Barrocal (➤ 67). For the adventurous, there are also many rough tracks for walking or cycling that quickly climb to heights of 400m or more around Vale Covo and Figueira Brava.

MONCARAPACHO ✪✪

This small, roadside town would be of little interest to visitors had not the local parish priest (who died in 1996) built up a remarkable small museum alongside the baroque Santo Cristo chapel (follow signs to 'Museu'). It is filled with a collection of curiosities that offer a profile of the history and archaeology of the whole region: there are coins, stones from an old olive press, shackles once used to imprison African slaves, Napoleonic cannon balls, and clay scoops from Moorish-style water wheels. Among the Roman masonry, there are soldier's tombstones and a milestone that once stood alongside the main road from Faro to Seville.

Upstairs, pride of place goes to a beautiful, 18th-century Neopolitan crib scene, with lively figures of shepherds and kings, made from wood and porcelain. Alongside the museum, the tiny 16th-century chapel is covered in 17th-century *azulejos*.

The main church in the town centre has an exceptional Renaissance façade carved with the Annunciation, St Peter and St Paul, and scenes from the Passion of Christ. Animated hunchbacked figures torment Christ as helmeted soldiers prepare to scourge him. The perfectly preserved Renaissance interior has classical columns, painted with swirling red and blue acanthus-leaf patterns.

✚ 29E2
✉ 8km northeast of Olhão
♿ Few
🍴 Cafés (£) around the main square
🚌 Buses from Olhão
🔄 Olhão (➤ 86)

Museu
🕐 Mon, Tue, Wed and Fri 11–3
✋ Moderate

Opposite and below:
*fishing is a core element
in the Algarvian economy*

MONTE GORDO ⭐⭐

Separated from the beach by a wide, café-lined avenue, the hotels of Monte Gordo look down on one of the Algarve's finest beaches – a vast, broad sweep of golden sand. Numerous seasonal seafood restaurants and cafés, housed in makeshift timber cabins, sit along the sands, offering fresh fish provided by the local fishermen.

With its warm waters, gentle offshore breezes and endless sands, Monte Gordo is a popular place for novice windsurfers to take their first tentative lessons, and there are plenty of beachside businesses offering watersports equipment and tuition. The nightlife is very lively and cosmopolitan, with folk dance evenings, a casino, and all-night Spanish discos. Spain is a short drive away across the road bridge that crosses the River Guadiana, and local tour agents offer day trips to Seville, about two hours' drive to the east.

OLHÃO ⭐⭐⭐

Olhão is, along with Portimão, the biggest of the Algarve's fishing ports, and the eastern end of the town is dominated by warehouses and canning factories. The fish market along the seafront, with its patterned brick walls and corner turrets, has been modernised to meet EU health regulations, but has lost none of its vital character. Equally colourful is the fruit and vegetable market, its stalls piled high with dried figs, almonds, honey, herbs and local cheeses, as well as fresh fruits.

On the opposite side of the seafront promenade Olhão divides into two distinct districts. To the east is a dense warren of narrow, cobbled alleys where the houses are North African in style – cube shaped, with undecorated façades and flat roofs. By contrast, the western half of the town has some of the Algarve's most attractive and ornate buildings, with curvaceous balconies, decorated with wrought-iron flowers and acorn finials. One fine group of buildings lines the same square that houses the tourist information centre, and there are more in the streets radiating north. These lead to the town's restored church, with its marvellously theatrical baroque façade. Inside, life-size angels flank the splendid, gilded altar. Shops and cafés line the pedestrianised Rua do Comércio, which leads from the church back to the seafront.

RESERVA NATURAL DA RIA FORMOSA (► 26, TOP TEN)

SÃO BRÁS DE ALPORTEL ⭐⭐

São Brás is a prosperous market town sandwiched between the the scenic Serra da Monte Figo region and the Serra do Caldeirão to the north. The area is renowned for its almond orchards, which blossom from late December to early March. A good spot from where to view the fertile countryside is the tombstone-flagged terrace of the largely rebuilt 15th-century church, which contains some lively 18th-century paintings and statues of the Archangel Gabriel and St Euphemia. Two blocks east of the church, the building that once served as the summer palace of the Bishops of Faro is fronted by an attractive domed pavilion, which shelters the eight-spouted Episcopal Fountain.

The **Museu Etnográfico do Traje Algarvio** (Algarvian Ethnographic Costume Museum) lies one block north in the former home of a wealthy 19th-century cork merchant. The displays of clothing, furniture and domestic objects illustrate various aspects of Algarvian rural life, and the farm buildings alongside house a collection of agricultural implements and old vehicles.

✚ 29E2
✉ 13km east of Loulé
🕐 Mon–Fri
🍴 Cafés (£) around Largo do Igreja and Largo do Mercado
🚌 Buses from Faro
ℹ Rua Dr Evaristo Sousa Gago 1 ☎ 089 842211
↔ Faro (➤ 62)

Museu Etnográfico do Traje Algarvio

✉ Rua Dr José Dias Sancho 59
☎ 089 842618
🕐 Mon–Fri 10–1, 2–5; Sat and Sun 2–5. Closed public hols
♿ Few
💷 Moderate

🚩 29F2

✉ At the eastern edge of the Algarve, 23km east of Tavira

🍴 Cafés (£) in Praça Marquês de Pombal and pedestrian streets north of the square

🚌 Bus station on Avenida Casal Ribeiro ☎ 081 511807 with services to and from Altura, Cacela, Castro Marim, Faro, Manta Rota, Monte Gordo, Olhão and Tavira

🔁 Castro Marim (➤ 82)

Ayamonte

🚩 29F2

✉ In Spain, on opposite bank of River Guadiana to Vila Real

🍴 Cafés (£) and restaurants (£) in Plaza de la Ligna

Museu Manuel Cabanas

✉ Praca Marquês de Pombal

🕐 Tue–Sun 11–12:30, 3–5. Closed Mon and public hols

VILA REAL DE SANTO ANTÓNIO ✪✪✪

Vila Real was founded by Royal Charter in 1773 and represents the town planning ideals of the Marquês de Pombal (1699–1782), Portugal's chief minister under King José I (1714–77). It was the Marquês, virtually exercising absolute power, who expelled the Jesuits from Portugal and swept away many church-based institutions. He planned this city to represent the rational ideals of the Enlightenment, in contrast to the Spanish city of Ayamonte on the opposite bank of the River Guadiana.

Ayamonte has prospered, as shown by its gleaming white tower blocks and modern port facilities, whilst charming Vila Real remains in a time warp. Vila's riverside embankment is lined by grand hotels and scores of restaurants and shops catering for the Spanish bargain hunters who come here to buy household goods, tempted by low prices and an advantageous exchange rate.

One block inland from the river embankment, the legacy of the Marquês is evident in the strict grid of streets and the geometrical precision of the elegant main square, Praça Marquês de Pombal, with its church, town hall and former infantry barracks. In the centre of the square, the obelisk monument to King José I acts like the needle of a giant sundial, casting its shadow on the black and white mosaic paving.

In 1991, a new suspension bridge opened across the River Guadiana, linking Portugal to Spain, but the river ferry continues to do a brisk trade, plying the river at roughly half-hourly intervals, from 9 until 9. You do not need a passport to visit **Ayamonte** (Spain and Portugal have abolished their common borders) and this is a good way of sampling the different cultures of the two countries (don't forget that Spain is usually an hour ahead of Portugal, and that almost everything shuts for the siesta, from 1 to 4).

By contrast with the monochrome Pombeline style of Vila Real, Ayamonte seems the more colourful town of the two, with its flower-filled streets and its lavishly tiled

Across the river from Vila Real, Ayamonte's white towers gleam

façades. It is also a town with many art galleries and studios displaying the work of contemporary artists, attracted by the lucid air and bold colours of the Costa del Luz (Coast of Light).

Ayamonte does not have the monopoly on 20th-century art, however. Back in Vila Real, the **Museu Manuel Cabanas** contains works by the eponymous local painter and engraver whose woodcuts of Algarvian life in the 1950s are very enjoyable. The same museum has a fascinating display of lithographic stones and designs for the labels used on locally canned sardines and pilchards – constituting a mini museum of packaging and advertising.

Did you know ?

Vila Real de Santo António was built in just five months, using the same techniques developed by the Marquês de Pombal in rebuilding Lisbon after the 1755 earthquake – building materials were brought to the site by boat, including timbers and masonry already cut and dressed, ready to use.

The Praça Marquês de Pombal, with its obelisk, resembles a giant sundial

Eastern Highlights

Distance
160km

Time
1 day

Start/end point
Tavira
✚ 29E2

Lunch
O Soeiro(£)
✉ Rua do Município 4,
    Alcoutim
☎ 081 546241

Cork oak, grown for its bark, flourishes in the hills of inland Algarve

Explore the empty hills of the Serra do Caldeirão, with their abandoned windmills and cork-oak forests, then follow the scenic Guadiana River.

From Tavira, head north on the EN 397 for 33km to Cachopo.

The countryside consists largely of shallow, acidic schistic soils that are not very fertile, though cork oaks thrive. In between the forests are hills covered in wild cistus and holly oak. Cachopo produces sheep's milk cheese and sweet, air-cured mountain hams.

Continue north on the EN 124 for 16km to Martim Longo, then south on the EN 506 for 12km to Vaqueiros.

Just south of Vaqueiros, visit the Cova dos Mouros mine, which was worked from the Copper Age (3500 BC) onwards and is now an industrial museum (➤ 82).

Continue a short way south, then turn left (east) and continue for 18km to the junction with the EN 122; head left (north) for 13km to the junction with the EN 124, then right (east) on the EN 124 for 6km to Alcoutim.

Stop for lunch in Alcoutim (➤ 80), then explore the castle.

Head south on the road that follows the River Guadiana.

Look out for the Roman ruins lying by the roadside just as you enter Montinho das Laranjeiras, immediately before the bridge; the remains consist of a villa and an early Christian church, with apse and stone-lined graves. In Guerreiros do Rio, stop to visit the former school, which now houses a small river museum.

When the river road meets the EN 122, turn left (south) and continue for 8km to Azinhal, noted for its lacework. Approaching Castro Marim (➤ 83), there are views to the left of the suspension bridge carrying the IP 1 motorway across the River Guadiana to Seville, in southern Andalucia. To return quickly to Tavira, join the motorway here and head west.

Where To...

Above: fado *singers*
Right: *typical* cataplana *dish*

Western Algarve

Prices
Prices are approximate, based on a three-course meal for one without drinks and service:

£ = under 2,000 escudos
££ = 2,000–3,500 escudos
£££ = over 3,500 escudos

Opening Hours
Most restaurants in the Algarve open from 10AM through to midnight, though smarter restaurants may close between 3 and 7, and some open only in the evening.

Barão de São João
Cangalho (££)
Rustic Portuguese cuisine is the speciality of this rural restaurant, located in a traditional farmhouse. The home-baked bread comes fresh from a wood-fired clay oven, as does the roast suckling pig, chicken *cabidela* and hunter's rabbit.
✉ Quinta Figueiras, Sitio do Medronho, Barão de São João ☎ 082 687218 🕔 Lunch, dinner. Closed Mon

Florestal (££)
Idyllically set in a forest of pine, mimosa and eucalyptus trees, the varied menu at this friendly restaurant reflects the English and American origins of the husband and wife owners – not least in the real 100 per cent beef American hamburgers served at lunchtime, with all the trimmings.
✉ Barão de São João, 3km west of Bensafrim ☎ 082 687204 🕔 Lunch, dinner. Closed Tue and Nov–Easter

Burgau
Ancora (££)
Enjoy sea views with your food, choosing from an adventurous menu: mussels cooked in Indian spices and pork in a fig sauce are among the imaginative offerings.
✉ Largo dos Pescadores ☎ 082 697102 🕔 Dinner. Closed Mon in summer, Mon and Tue in winter

Beach Bar (£)
Rock-bottom prices at this well-positioned beachside restaurant, with its seafront terrace, specialising in grilled fresh fish.
✉ Praia de Burgau ☎ 082 697553 🕔 Lunch, dinner. Closed Mon

Cabeça do Porco (Pig's Head) (££)
The porcine theme is reflected in the décor of this English-style pub, and in the very popular pig roasts, served on Sundays. Portuguese, English and international dishes are on the menu during the rest of the week.
✉ Luz road, east of Burgau ☎ 082 697315 🕔 Lunch, dinner

Caravela (£££)
Up-market Portuguese cuisine, served in the attractive surroundings of a palm-shaded garden. Rabbit hunter-style, and roast saddle of lamb cooked in mountain herbs are popular.
✉ Rua Direita ☎ 082 69274 🕔 Dinner

Casa Grande (££)
Set in the former winery attached to a beautifully restored manor house, this restaurant has Portuguese and vegetarian dishes to suite all tastes. Reservations advised.
✉ On the Burgau to Praia da Luz road ☎ 082 697416 🕔 Dinner. Closed Dec–Feb

Rios Negros (£££)
The owner-chef at this deservedly popular restaurant also catches the fresh fish that are grilled over a charcoal brazier. Grilled meats available too. Drawings and photographs of local artists decorate the walls.
✉ Largo do Poço 4, Vale de Boi, on the EN 125 between

Burgau and Budens ☎ 082 695330 🕐 Dinner. Closed Mon

Lagos
A Capoeira (££)
The 'Chicken Coop' does not limit its menu to grilled fowl: you can also choose from a range of Portuguese regional meat and fish dishes, or the colonial-style 'pork Mozambique'.
✉ Rua 25 de Abril ☎ No phone 🕐 Lunch, dinner

Alpendre (£££)
Good fish and seafood in a characterful setting just off the town's main square.
✉ Rua António Barbarosa Viana 17 ☎ 082 762705 🕐 Lunch, dinner

Dom Sebastião (££)
This popular restaurant, with its timbered ceiling, also has an open-air terrace and an extensive menu.
✉ Rua 25 de Abril ☎ 082 762795 🕐 Lunch, dinner. Closed Sun in winter

Mediterraneo (££)
Vegetarians will find plenty of choice at this friendly restaurant with a shady terrace.
✉ Rua da Senhora da Graça ☎ 082 768476 🕐 Lunch, dinner

O Pátio (££)
Scandinavian and Portuguese dishes vie for attention on the menu of this beautiful old town-house restaurant, with its peaceful patio garden.
✉ Rua Lançarote de Freitas 46 ☎ 082 763777 🕐 Dinner. Closed Mon all year and Sun and Mon Nov–May

Sambal (££)
A rare find anywhere, this restaurant serves excellent Indonesian cuisine, including multi-course *rijstaffel* banquets, vegetarian dishes and Balinese satay. Some Thai dishes as well.
✉ Rua de Santa Isabel ☎ 082 422072 🕐 Dinner. Closed Thu

Praia da Luz
Fortaleza da Luz (££)
The remains of the town's 16th-century fortress have been turned into a popular and characterful restaurant with good coastal views. Fresh fish, Portuguese cuisine and flambé dishes, plus live jazz on Sundays.
✉ Rua da Igreja 3 ☎ 082 789926 🕐 Lunch, dinner. Closed mid-Nov to mid-Dec

Sagres
A Tasca (££)
Located on the harbour in Sagres, in a building that once served as a market, and specialising in fresh fish, including lobster and clams *amêijoas*.
✉ Sagres harbour ☎ 082 624177 🕐 Lunch, dinner

Bossa Nova (£)
Pasta and pizzas, plus vegetarian dishes and seafood at this friendly and moderately priced restaurant.
✉ Rua da Mareta ☎ 082 624566 🕐 Lunch, dinner

Fortaleza do Beliche (££)
An up-market Portuguese restaurant located in the atmospheric setting of a fortress destroyed by Sir Francis Drake in 1587 and restored in the 1960s.
✉ 5km southeast of Sagres on the road to Cabo de São Vicente ☎ 082 624124 🕐 Lunch, dinner

Pousada do Infante (££)
Luxuriate in the comfortable ambience of this hotel restaurant serving locally caught fish, set on a cliff-top with sweeping views.
✉ Atalaia Point ☎ 082 624222 🕐 Lunch, dinner

Bars and *Pastelarias*
Bars are usually open all day, from early in the morning until late at night, serving coffee, soft drinks and alcohol. Most serve cheese, ham or *presunto* (cured ham) sandwiches, and there will usually be a small display of cakes. Just about every village, no matter how small, has a bar, so you are never very far from refreshment. The *pastelaria* is one step up: usually attached to a bakery, it serves a much more extensive range of cakes, as well as savoury snacks, such as quiche or salads, hot dogs and hamburgers. More often found in towns and cities than in villages, the *pastelaria* is where many city-dwellering Portuguese eat lunch, and most close at 7, as the restaurants begin to open.

Appetisers
When you eat in an Algarvian restaurant, the waiter will present you with a basket of delicious home-made bread, along with a selection of spreads – butter, cheese and sardine paste are the commonest – which many Portuguese will have instead of a starter. Some restaurants also serve home-cured olives and a range of nibbles – such as chopped vegetables dressed with garlic, herbs and oil – which make a delicious accompaniment to pre-dinner drinks.

93

Western Central Algarve

Fish on the Menu

Your favourite fish may not seem so familiar if the menu only has their names in Portuguese. Here is a short list of fish that you will frequently find on Algarvian menus: *atum* (tuna), *bacalhau* (salted cod), *cherne* (sea bass), *carapau* (mackerel), *pargo* (bream), *salmão* (salmon), *salmonete* (red mullet), *truta* (trout) and *espadarte* (swordfish).

Alvor

Somewhere Else (££)
Fun restaurant with Irish and Dutch owners where you get to cook your own meat or fresh fish on heated lava stones.

⊠ **Rua Poeta João de Deus** ☎ **082 458595** 🕙 **Lunch, dinner**

Caldas de Monchique

Restaurante Central (£)
A popular spot for a leisurely lunch, this elegant building is redolent of the spa town in its fashionable heyday. Try the locally produced mountain ham, or the house speciality, *bacalhau á Central* (salt cod with a mushroom and cream sauce).

⊠ **Off the central square** ☎ **082 912203** 🕙 **Lunch, dinner**

Carvoeiro

Grande Muralha (££)
This Sino-Portuguese restaurant has familiar and not-so-familiar dishes on its menu, including curried squid, delicious sizzling prawns, and fried ice-cream.

⊠ **Estrada do Farol, Praia do Carvoeiro** ☎ **082 357380** 🕙 **Lunch, dinner**

Ferragudo

A Lanterna (££)
Try the lamb marinaded in garlic and herbs, and the delicious range of local almond-based desserts.

⊠ **At the junction of the EN 125 and the Ferragudo road** ☎ **082 423948** 🕙 **Lunch, dinner. Closed Sun**

Lagoa

Casa Velha (££)
Come here on a Saturday night for live *fado* music, but be sure to book in advance. Set in a converted bakery, adorned by the paintings of the owner's artist wife, this popular restaurant serves African-influenced dishes, such as Angolan prawns and chicken moamba, alongside Algarvian staples.

⊠ **Rua Mouzinho de Albuquerque 60** ☎ **082 342600** 🕙 **Lunch, dinner**

Monchique

Água da Sola (£)
Good-value roadside restaurant between Monchique and Fóia serving chicken *piri-piri* and various kebabs to hungry walkers.

⊠ **Estrada da Fóia** ☎ **No phone** 🕙 **Lunch, dinner**

Bica-Boa (££)
The owners have transformed this traditional restaurant on the Lisbon road into one of the Algarve's best restaurants, serving good regional and international food.

⊠ **Estrada de Lisboa** ☎ **082 912271** 🕙 **Lunch, dinner**

Paraíso da Montanha (£)
Visitors flock to this restaurant on the Fóia road for its excellent chicken *piri-piri*, and for the mountain views from the terrace.

⊠ **Estrada da Fóia** ☎ **082 912150** 🕙 **Lunch, dinner**

Quinta de São Bento (£££)
The views from this award-winning restaurant vie for attention with the grandeur of the building – the former summer residence of the royal House of Bragança – located near the summit of Fóia, the Algarve's highest peak. Wild boar, rabbit, hare,

partridge and pheasant feature on a menu that specialises in game.

✉ Estrada da Fóia ☎ 082 912143 🕐 Lunch, dinner

Portimão
Dona Barca (£)
One of the best of Portimão's renowned fish restaurants, located in a converted riverside warehouse and serving fish straight off the boats, including sea bass, bream, seafood rice and *cataplana* (fish stew). Live music in summer.

✉ Largo da Barca ☎ 082 484189 🕐 Lunch, dinner

O Cantinho (£)
In a town renowned for its sardine restaurants, this one allows you to eat as much as you like for a bargain all-in price of 400 escudos.

✉ Rua Dr João Vitorino Mealha ☎ No phone 🕐 Lunch, dinner

O Refúgio (The Haven) (£)
Portuguese meets British in this family-friendly restaurant much patronised by English expats, where Algarvian favourites, such as chicken *piri-piri*, feature alongside liver and onions or prawn curry. Vegetarian selection and children's menu.

✉ Rua João Eanes 35 ☎ 082 426272 🕐 Lunch, dinner. Closed Sun

Salfino (£)
Mexican food: pick and choose from the usual range of *nachos*, *tacos*, *burritos* and *fajitas*, or try the vegetarian dishes.

✉ Praça 1 de Maio ☎ No phone 🕐 Lunch, dinner

Praia da Rocha
Cabassa (££)
Enjoy Thai beef in coconut sauce and various oriental seafood dishes at this seafront restaurant, with an extensive terrace.

✉ Avenida Tomás Cabreira ☎ 082 424307 🕐 Lunch, dinner. Closed Nov–Mar

Churrasqueira (£)
Spicy chicken *piri-piri* at good-value prices draws diners to this busy cliff-top restaurant.

✉ Avenida Tomás Cabreira ☎ 082 417452 🕐 Lunch, dinner

Shang Hai (££)
One of two restaurants in Praia da Rocha that will appeal to lovers of Chinese food (the sister restaurant is the Bamboo Garden, Loja 1, Edifício Lamego, Avenida Tomás Cabreira). Both restaurants make the most of the fresh local seafood and have an extensive menu of traditional Chinese dishes. Deep-fried ice-cream is the signature dish.

✉ Loja 2, Edifício Cruzeiro ☎ 082 416601 🕐 Lunch, dinner

Silves
Café Inglês (£)
Located opposite the cathedral and alongside the castle entrance, this café is set in an elegant 1920s house originally built as the residence of the mayor. Enjoy home-baked bread and cakes with afternoon tea or more substantial Portuguese and English-style snacks.

✉ Escadas do Castello 11 ☎ 082 442585 🕐 Lunch, dinner. Closed Sat

Casa Velha de Silves (££)
Overshadowed by the gates to the old Moorish city, the Casa Velha offers traditional Portuguese grilled fish, *cataplana* (fish stew) and *espetada* (kebabs). Regular concerts of *fado* and other folk music are held in the basement bar.

✉ Rua 25 de Abril 13 ☎ 082 445491 🕐 Lunch, dinner

Accompaniments
You do not normally need to order vegetables or salad separately with your main course. The dish will automatically be served with a selection of cooked seasonal vegetables, or a small salad of grated carrots and cabbage, with tomato and cucumber. Chips are the traditional accompaniment to meat dishes, and boiled potatoes are served with fish, unless you request otherwise.

Eastern Central Algarve

Algarvian Wine

Local wines are very cheap and quite strong – especially the reds, which are typically 13 or 13.5% alcohol. They are sold mostly as *vinho da casa* and, in traditional Portuguese restaurants, are drawn from a barrel. If you want a bottle of local wine, look for the Lagoa label. Wine experts tend to dismiss Algarvian wines, saying they lack subtlety. Softer and fuller flavoured wines come from the Alentejo, and are sold under the names of the co-operative producers, Borba, Redondo and Reguengos de Monsaraz.

Albufeira

O Penedo (££)
Delicious garlic clams are the speciality of this popular beachside restaurant.
✉ Rua Latino Coelho 15
☎ 089 587429 🕐 Lunch, dinner

Phillippos (££)
Try Greek for a change. Traditional lamb dishes, salads and moussaka plus dancing and plate-smashing – fun but noisy.
✉ Montechoro Park, alongside the Montechoro Hotel
☎ 0936 838193 🕐 Lunch, dinner. Closed Sun

Almancil

Adega Cova (£)
Simple restaurant specialising in *cabrito estufado* (casseroled and roast kid), served with the owner's homemade wine.
✉ Vale d'Águas ☎ 089 395281 🕐 Lunch, dinner

Chameleon (££)
Youthful, fun pub with live Irish music and theme parties, serving a range of meals and bar snacks, including steaks and all-American burgers.
✉ Rua da República 40 ☎ No phone 🕐 Lunch, dinner

La Paella (££)
If you have tried *arroz do marisco* (Portuguese seafood rice), come here to find out how it compares with paella. For those with smaller appetites, the restaurant serves a range of *tapas*, including delicious spicy prawns, fried mushrooms and vegetables with various dips.
✉ Estrada de Vale d'Aguas 26
☎ 089 393874 🕐 Lunch, dinner

Alte

Alte Hotel (££)
Unbroken views of the limestone hills of the Barrocal region, and a menu that features an extensive choice of local fish and seafood dishes. Given 24 hours' notice, they will produce typically Algarvian dishes, such as pig's trotters with beans and spicy sausage.
✉ On the road from Alte to Santa Margarida ☎ 089 68523 🕐 Lunch, dinner

Faro

Aliança (£)
The food is unexciting and the service slow at this traditional Portuguese café, one of the oldest in the country, but people come for the ambience of the dimly lit, wood-panelled 1920s interior, and to sit where statesmen and philosophers, including Simone de Beauvoir, have sat.
✉ Praça Francisco Gomes 6
☎ 089 801621 🕐 Lunch

Bella Italia (£)
Good Italian eatery at the harbour end of the main shopping street, offering authentic pizzas in a wood-fired clay oven.
✉ Rua Dr Francisco Gomes
☎ 089 826701 🕐 Lunch, dinner

Cidade Velha (££)
Atmospheric town-house restaurant in the old city close to the cathedral and archaeological museum. Imaginative menu includes fresh clams steamed with coriander, dates wrapped in bacon, and prawns in beer.
✉ Rua Domingos Guieiro 19
☎ 089 27145 🕐 Lunch, dinner

Clube Naval (££)

With the harbour on one side and the railway on the other, there is plenty to see from the windows of the nautically themed Clube Naval, which specialises in fish and pork *cataplana* with cockles.

✉ Doca de Faro ☎ 089 823869 🕐 Lunch

Piri Piri da Costa (£)

The name says it all – chicken *piri-piri* with views of the coast from the long, sandy barrier reef that serves as Faro's beach.

✉ Praia de Faro ☎ 089 817442 🕐 Lunch, dinner. Closed Tue

Loulé

Bicavelha (£££)

Located in a characterful medieval building, claimed to be the oldest in Loulé, this excellent restaurant has a varied menu of local fish, served with style. Reservations recommended.

✉ Rua Martim Moniz 17–19 ☎ 089 463376 🕐 Dinner

O Avenida Velha (££)

Distinguished and stately old restaurant, famous for its homemade bread, and a wide range of delicious, small savoury dishes, similar to Spanish *tapas*.

✉ Avenida José da Costa Mealha 40, First floor ☎ 089 416474 🕐 Lunch, dinner. Closed Sun

Quarteira

Adedga do Peixe (£)

Spacious, good-value restaurant specialising in charcoal-grilled sea food and typical Portuguese dishes.

✉ Avenida Infante de Sagres ☎ 089 388370 🕐 Lunch, dinner

O Infante (££)

Seafront restaurant popular with Portuguese holiday-makers for its shellfish and *cataplana* (fish stew).

✉ Avenida Infante de Sagres 131 ☎ 089 313576 🕐 Lunch, dinner

Sea Horse (£)

Good-value family restaurant run by friendly Dutch owners, with savoury and sweet pancakes on the menu, alongside more traditional fish dishes.

✉ Avenida Infante de Sagres ☎ 089 313074 🕐 Lunch, dinner

Querença

Restaurante de Querença (££)

Set in the main square of this tiny hilltop village, looking over to the gleaming, white baroque parish church in one direction and the foothills of the Serra do Caldeirão in the other, this restaurant is an excellent choice for whiling away the long siesta hours, or enjoying a dinner with traditional accordion music at weekends. Rabbit and wild boar appear on the menu in various guises, as well as fish kebabs and lamb dishes. Reservations recommended at weekends.

✉ Largo da Igreja ☎ 089 422540 🕐 Lunch, dinner. Closed Wed

Vale do Lobo

Memories of China (£££)

The Algarve branch of the late Ken Lo's famous chain of up-market Chinese restaurants. Faultless and memorable food, including the delicious sizzling three-seafood platter.

✉ David Lloyd Tennis Centre, Vale do Lobo ☎ 089 393939 🕐 Dinner. Closed Sat

Vilamoura

Golden Ming (££)

Very popular Chinese restaurant alongside the yacht-filled marina – booking is essential in summer.

✉ Marina Plaza ☎ 089 301082 🕐 Lunch, dinner

Desserts

Two desserts that you will invariably find on the menu are *tarte* and *pudim*. *Tarte* can be made with many different ingredients, but nearly all have ground almonds as their base, mixed with flour and egg, poured into a pastry case and baked until golden. Some are additionally flavoured with lemon juice or honey syrup. *Pudim* is crème caramel, but not the individual servings you might expect in a French restaurant: Portuguese *pudim* is a substantial ring of steamed egg custard from which slices are cut to order. A more unusual choice, if you can find it, is *queijo de figo* – literally 'fig cheese' – made from layers of dried figs, ground almonds, cinnamon and chocolate.

Eastern Algarve

Regional Variations

In coastal regions, grilled fresh fish predominates, and regular deliveries to even the most distant inland village means that it is also a major element on their menus, though not in such great variety. Inland you are more likely to find lamb, kid, pork and chicken, while restaurants in the Barrocal mountains will often have a section of the menu devoted to game: wild boar, quail, partridge, hare and rabbit in particular. Perhaps the most distinctive cuisine is that of the Guadiana River valley, where the river itself is the source of the eels, lampreys and mullet that are typical of local restaurants.

Alcoutim
O Soeiro (£)
Tucked into a shady corner beside the parish church, O Soeiro is frequented by local ferrymen waiting for passengers wanting to cross to Spain. From tables on the terrace there are river views, and you can watch your chicken or pork being grilled over a charcoal brazier.
✉ Rua do Município 4 ☎ 081 546241 🕐 Lunch. Closed Sat and Sun

Barranco do Velho
A Tia Bia (££)
This fine restaurant is often packed with hungry walkers and cyclists who come to enjoy the rare landscape of the forested Serra do Caldeirão mountains. Specialising in game dishes, you are likely to find wild boar on the menu, as well as partridge with cabbage, and pumpkin with rabbit.
✉ Barranco do Velho crossroads ☎ 089 846425 🕐 Lunch, dinner

Guerreiros do Rio
O Caleiro (£)
Characterful restaurant specialising in fish from the River Guadiana, including lamprey, eel and mullet.
✉ Rua Guerreiros do Rio ☎ 081 547103 🕐 Lunch, dinner. Closed Mon

Monte Gordo
Dourado (££)
One of a group of timber shacks on the beach at Monte Gordo, with shaded terraces serving *cataplana* and a wide range of other traditional Portuguese dishes.
✉ Avenida Infante Dom Henrique ☎ 081 512202 🕐 Lunch, dinner

Goa (££)
Southern Indian food majoring in delicate fish curries with coconut and fruits.
✉ Rua Fernando Pó ☎ 081 512606 🕐 Dinner

Santa Bárbara de Nexe
La Réserve (£££)
Much-lauded restaurant, regarded by some as the Algarve's best. Mainly French food served stylishly, but at a high price. Reservations essential in summer.
✉ Estrada de Esteval ☎ 089 999234 🕐 Lunch, dinner. Closed Tue

São Brás de Aportel
Pousada de São Brás (££)
Elegant restaurant in state-run hotel with beautiful views over wooded hills. Try *caldeirada de borrego* (lamb stew).
✉ São Brás de Aportel ☎ 089 843205 🕐 Lunch, dinner

Luís dos Frangos (£)
Locals flock here for the mouth-watering barbecued chicken, served with chips, salad and local wine.
✉ Tavira road ☎ No phone 🕐 Lunch, dinner

Tavira
Beira Rio (££)
By the old bridge, this elegant riverside restaurant has a good range of vegetarian dishes and is noted for its garlic-flavoured quail. Booking recommended in summer.
✉ Rua Borda d'Água da Assêca 46–52 ☎ 081 323165 🕐 Lunch, dinner. Closed last three weeks in Nov and Jan–Easter

Bica (£)
Plain and simple, but friendly atmosphere and huge portions. Try *corvina à casa* (bream in onion sauce).

✉ Rua Almirante Cândido dos Reis 22–24 (in the Residencial Lagôas) ☎ 081 323843 ⏱ Lunch, dinner

Casa Cota (£)
Dine on the roof terrace for views over the characterful roof tops of Tavira. Specialises in charcoal-grilled meats.

✉ Rua João Vaz Corte Real 38 ☎ 081 324873 ⏱ Lunch, dinner

Imperial (£££)
Grand restaurant renowned for its chicken and rice dishes, and its *serrabucho de marisco* (mixed seafood with pork).

✉ Rua José Pires Padinha 22 ☎ 081 322306 ⏱ Lunch, dinner

Mares (££)
Friendly restaurant with pavement tables along the Gilão River embankment, alongside the Tavira Island ferry point. Good regional cooking and flambé dishes.

✉ Rua José Pires Padinha 134–40 ☎ 081 325815 ⏱ Lunch, dinner

Marisqueira 4 Águas (££)
It is a short step from the boat to the table for the fish and shellfish served at this atmospheric restaurant, located alongside the fish warehouse, at the junction of the rivers Gilão and Formosa.

✉ Quatro Águas ☎ 081 325329 ⏱ Lunch, dinner

O Pátio (££)
Push the boat out and try lobster or tiger prawns flambé, or sample something more modestly priced, such as clams *cataplana*, couscous or fish kebab, washed down with the local Taviran wine.

✉ Rua António Cabreira 30 ☎ 081 323008 ⏱ Lunch, dinner

Patricks (£)
Irish pub, on the opposite side of the street to O Pátio, serving draught Murphy's and various other beers and ciders. Bar snacks include filling and inexpensive chilli con carne, chicken *piri-piri* and several vegetarian dishes.

✉ Rua António Cabreira 30 ☎ No phone ⏱ Lunch, dinner

Vila Real de Santo António
Caves do Guadiana (££)
Located on the banks of the Guadiana River, this restaurant specialises in Portuguese-style seafood and spicy African-style cod.

✉ Avenida da República 89 ☎ 081 544498 ⏱ Lunch, dinner. Closed Thu dinner

O Curação de Cidade (££)
Large and popular with tables spilling on to the pavement of the pedestrianised shopping street west of the main square. The vast menu caters to the tastes of many nationalities, from English sandwiches to Spanish *tapas* by way of Andalucian *gazpacho* and squid 'Sevilhana', plus pizzas and chicken *piri-piri*.

✉ Rua Cândido dos Reis ☎ 081 512972 ⏱ Lunch, dinner

Liqueurs
Algarvians have a gift for turning their local fruits into alcoholic liqueurs. The most popular drink with which to end the meal is *medronho*, a potent spirit distilled from the strawberry-coloured fruits of the arbutus tree, which grows in profusion in the Monchique region. Lovers of almonds will adore the delicious sweet liqueur called *amêndoa amarga*, also sold as *Algarviana*. Another good choice is *brandymel*, a warming blend of brandy and honey.

Western Algarve

Prices

Prices are for a double room, including breakfast and tax:

£ = under 7,500 escudos

££ = 7,500–15,000 escudos

£££ = over 15,000 escudos

Hotels

Many seafront hotels in the Algarve are of a very high standard, with luxurious accommodation in well-maintained gardens, overlooking a glorious beach. They are also quite expensive, though often cheaper if booked as part of a package holiday. Conversely, tour companies often charge more for the cheaper hotels than if you booked direct. Nearly all hotels in the Algarve include breakfast as part of the room price. Half- and full-board terms are also available at the more expensive hotels.

Burgau

Casa Grande (£)

This characterful guest house is packed with antiques and collectables. Artists and writers love its faded grandeur and so will anyone searching for something different from the run-of-the-mill modern hotel.

✉ 8650 Burgau ☎ 082 697416
🕐 Closed Dec–Feb

Lagos

Golfinho (££)

Superb views of the Dona Ana beach, with its wind-sculpted rocks, from this modern 4-star hotel, with pool, restaurant and bar.

✉ Praia Dona Ana ☎ 082 769900 🕐 All year

Hotel de Lagos (££)

Enjoy the bustling life of the western Algarve's biggest town at this airy hotel, a few minutes' walk from the centre. Facilities include indoor swimming pool and jacuzzi, and regular transport to the beach.

✉ Rua Nova da Aldeia ☎ 082 769967 🕐 All year

Praia da Luz

Belavista (££)

Many people return to this quiet resort again and again because it combines the best of the Algarve – sandy beaches, glorious walking and good restaurants. The Belavista sits above the sheltered beach at Praia da Luz, with its rooms grouped amphitheatre-style around the central swimming pool. The rooms are spacious and comfortable and there is plenty to do here, from scuba diving and discos for the teenagers to yoga and meditation classes.

✉ Beach road, Praia da Luz ☎ 082 788655 🕐 All year

Luz Bay Club (££)

As an alternative to hotel accommodation, the Luz Bay Club makes an excellent choice, with two-, three- and four-bedroomed villas for visitors who prefer the self-catering option, but with a restaurant and other amenities on hand. There is an adults-only pool and a fun pool with slide, tennis and squash courts, restaurant and bar, and watersports facilities, including dinghy sailing, windsurfing and scuba diving.

✉ Avenida Pescadores, Praia da Luz, 8600 Lagos ☎ 082 788553 🕐 All year

Sagres

Fortaleza do Beliche (££)

You have to book well in advance to stay at this *pousada* (state-run hotel), but advance planning is worth it to enjoy the charm and character of this 16th-century fortress, sacked by Sir Francis Drake in 1587 and restored in the 1960s. Set on a cliff-top, there are wonderful views to enjoy with your meals on the terrace.

✉ 8650 Sagres ☎ 082 624124 🕐 All year

Pousada do Infante (££)

Located on the cliff-tops, this splendid *pousada* (state-run hotel) is built in traditional Algarvian style, with red-tiled roofs, ornate chimneys and a cloister-like loggia providing shaded terraces to its rooms. Facilities include a swimming pool and tennis courts, and there is fishing and watersports in Sagres.

✉ 8650 Sagres ☎ 082 64222 🕐 All year

Western Central Algarve

Armação de Pêra
Vila Vita Parc (£££)

Architecturally, this is one of the more distinguished hotels in the Algarve, with its Moorish-inspired domes and shady cloisters, all set in a huge and beautifully planted tropical water garden, with echoes of the Alhambra in Seville. The rooms are dotted around the grounds in a series of linked buildings, including some self-contained villas. Facilities include three outdoor swimming pools, a heated indoor pool for cooler weather, two children's pools and a Kids' Park children's playground, as well as tennis and squash courts, a 9-hole pitch and putt golf course, health club and beauty salon. There are five restaurants and a nightclub.

✉ Apartado 196, P-8365 Armação de Pêra ☎ 082 315310 🕔 All year

Carvoeiro
Almansor (££)

Well located for a number of golf courses, the Almansor is sited on the cliff-tops above its own cove, sheltered by sandstone cliffs and reached by a path from the hotel grounds. The hotel is built in ziggurat style, to ensure the best possible sea views from its rooms. Facilities include a pool, shops and a babysitting service.

✉ Praia Vale Covo, Carvoeiro, 8400 Lagoa ☎ 082 358026 🕔 All year

Ferragudo
Casabela Hotel (£££)

Luxurious hotel in a picturesque setting above the Praia Grande beach in an area that makes an excellent base for walking and watersports. Facilities include outdoor swimming pool heated all year round, tennis courts and restaurant with panoramic views.

✉ Vale da Areia, Ferragudo, near Portimão ☎ 082 461580 🕔 All year

Portimão
Le Meridien Penina (£££)

The perfect family resort hotel, the Penina offers supervised activities for children in July and August at the self-contained Penguin Club village, including excursions, competitions, tennis, golf, mountain biking and horse riding. Parents can take their pick of watersports, golf, tennis and horse riding, under the instruction of qualified experts. The accommodation is of the highest standard, with restaurants and a huge pool set in tree-shaded grounds.

✉ Apartado 146, Montes de Alvor, 8502 Portimão ☎ 082 415500 🕔 All year

Praia da Rocha
Algarve Casino (£££)

This is one of the Algarve's best hotels, with a huge range of facilities on offer, though at a price. The hotel sits on the cliff-top right above Praia da Rocha beach, and many of the rooms have balconies overlooking the ocean below. There are two heated outdoor pools, plus tennis courts and facilities for windsurfing and jet-skiing. The Praia da Rocha casino is part of the complex, with a restaurant and nightly dinner dances and floor shows.

✉ Praia da Rocha, 8500 Portimão ☎ 082 415001 🕔 All year

Self-catering

Most accommodation in the Algarve is in self-catering villas and apartments, often set in a complex around pleasant gardens, with central facilities such as a bar, swimming pool, shop and restaurant. Villas usually have a small kitchen with fridge and gas cooker, a garage and small garden, a living room with TV and simply furnished bedrooms with en suite bathrooms. A maid will clean the villa and change the linen once a week. Advance booking is essential for the main holiday period.

(Travel agents' brochures are full of offers, but you can often get a higher standard of accommodation, and better prices, by renting privately.)

Eastern Central & Eastern Algarve

Eastern Central Algarve

Albufeira

Aldeia (£)
Comfortable, modern, 3-star hotel forming part of a villa and apartment complex about 1.5km from the beach, with pool, children's pool, playground, disco, live music most nights, satellite TV, mini-golf and tennis.
✉ Avenida Dr Francisco Sá Carneiro 1, Areias de São João, 8200 Albufeira ☎ 089 588864 🄲 All year

Sheraton Algarve (£££)
Recently awarded Portugal's coveted Silver Medal for excellence in tourism services, the Sheraton Algarve, also known as Pinecliffs, is not just a hotel – it is a complete resort, with its own 9-hole golf course and golf academy, as well as a large outdoor pool and tennis-courts. Guests have access to miles of unbroken sand, with the beaches of Praia da Falésia right on the doorstep. Windsurfing, pedalos, jetskis and waterski facilities are all available, and there is a good choice of both casual and more formal restaurants.
✉ Praia da Falésia, 8200 Albufeira ☎ 089 501999 🄲 All year

Vila Joya (£££)
All the rooms at Vila Joya have sea views and are all luxuriously decorated, with mosaic-tiled bathrooms and tasteful furnishings. This exclusive hideaway is located well away from other developments, with access to the Praia de Galé beach, a heated pool, and facilities for fishing, sailing, windsurfing,

scuba diving, horse riding, tennis and golf. Guests are expected to stay for a minimum of one week.
✉ Praia de Galé ☎ 089 591795 🄲 Closed mid-Nov to mid-Dec, mid-Jan to mid-Feb

Almancil

Quinta do Lago (£££)
Set in 800 hectares of wild and undulating coastline on the Ria Formosa estuary, each room at Quinta do Lago has a garden terrace for a leisurely breakfast. Facilities inside the hotel complex include tennis courts, outdoor and indoor swimming pools, gym, sauna, solarium, masseuse, snooker on the premises, and two golf courses alongside. The hotel hires out bicycles and arranges fishing trips, waterskiing and windsurfing, sailing and canoeing.
✉ 8135 Almancil ☎ 089 396666 🄲 All year

Quinta dos Amigos (££)
Spend a week on a typical Portuguese farm and learn to ride or improve your horse riding finesse. The Quinta dos Amigos is ideal for families with older children. There are good beaches near by, and the watersports, discos, restaurants and golf courses of Vale do Lobo and Quinta do Lago are 10 minutes' drive away. Qualified instructors organise rural rides or canters along the beach. The self-catering accommodation consists of apartments in converted farm buildings, decorated with bright Algarvian textiles and painted antique furniture.
✉ Escanxinas, 8135 Almancil ☎ 089 395269 🄲 All year

Alte
Alte Hotel (££)

Many of the people who come here are walkers, taking advantage of the village's central location to explore the fascinating Barrocal countryside, with its limestone caves, cliffs and valleys and unspoiled Portuguese way of life. The hotel sits on a hill above Alte with views that stretch for miles towards the coast, a 45-minute drive away. Rooms are simple but comfortable, and facilities include tennis courts and a swimming pool, plus a restaurant specialising in fresh fish, game and rural Portuguese dishes such as pigs' trotters.

✉ Montino, Alte, 8100 Loulé
☎ 089 68523 🕑 All year

Vale do Lobo
Le Meridien
Dona Filipa (£££)

Part of the manicured and prestigious Vale do Lobo estate, the Dona Filipa enjoys a privileged position beside the Atlantic, a few feet from the beach and surrounded by golf courses – guests enjoy discounted green fees and an early start at the São Lourenço Club, rated one of the best in Europe. There are three floodlit tennis courts and a heated outdoor swimming pool to enjoy, as well as the tranquillity of this relatively small, elegant hotel. The two restaurants pride themselves on their wine lists.

✉ Vale do Lobo, 8136 Almancil
☎ 089 394141 🕑 All year

Vilamoura
Dom Pedro Marina (££)

Set back one block from the Vilamoura marina, the Dom Pedro is at the hub of this buzzing resort and within walking distance of all the marina's restaurants and nightlife. There are two pools, one for adults and one for children, plus an Italian restaurant. Babysitting can be arranged.

✉ Vilamoura, 8125 Quarteira
☎ 089 389802 🕑 All year

Eastern Algarve

São Brás de Alportel
Pousada São Brás (££)

Set in the peaceful foothills of São Brás de Alportel, this state-run hotel, part of Portugal's *pousada* chain, was built in 1944 but has been modernised and upgraded. The rooms are decorated in typical Algarvian style, and the facilities include a swimming pool and tennis court.

✉ 8150 São Brás de Alportel
☎ 01 848 1221 🕑 All year

Vila Real de Santo António
Hotel Guadiana (£)

This grand, historic hotel is classed as a national monument, and its turn-of-the-century décor includes frescoed walls, elegant marble statues of langorous female nudes and delightfully decorated rooms. Some rooms look across the River Guadiana to Spain and the ferry to Ayamonte leaves from the opposite side of the road. Seville and Granada are within driving distance and the long, sandy beaches of Monte Gordo are only 5 minutes away.

✉ Avenida da República 94, Vila Real de Santo António, 8900 Monte Gordo ☎ 081 511482
🕑 All year

Gradings and Prices

Hotels in the Algarve are graded from 1 to 5 stars, but there is considerable variation between the cost of a 3-star hotel on the coast, for example, and one in a less tourist-visited inland town – prices drop rapidly once you move away from the coast. For rock-bottom prices, look out for the simple *pensão* or residential guest houses, often in town centres, offering clean, no-frills accommodation. Above this, a 3-star hotel will probably consist of a modern, purpose-built block, with clean and comfortable rooms and en suite bathrooms, a restaurant and small pool. Buildings with greater character may style themselves as an *estalagem* or *albergeria*, and anything styled as a *quinta* is probably a luxurious converted manor house, at the centre of its own expansive estate.

103

Shopping in the Algarve

Loulé's Gypsy Market
If you want the best combination of permanent market and gypsy market, go to Loulé on a Saturday. Head for the Moorish-style building in Avenida José da Costa Mealha. Here, every street in the vicinity of the covered market has its smallholders, from farmers with sacks of grain and animal feed to souvenir stalls piled with painted cockerels and plates. For gourmets, there is a delightful range of home-produced food on sale, including herb-marinated olives, dried figs, almond-based sweets, bundles of dried spices, sweet cheeses, hams and spicy sausages.

Permanent Markets

Every town of any size has a permanent covered market which opens every day except Sunday from 6:30AM, and which stays open until around 1PM, though the later you arrive, the less choice there will be. Markets are being upgraded to comply with EU hygiene standards, but this has been achieved without destroying their character.

There are usually separate areas for wet fish and for fruit and vegetables, and some have butcher's shops in separate premises around the perimeter of the market hall. Larger markets also have stalls selling delicious home-baked bread, mountain-cured ham and local sheep's-milk cheeses. Markets attract gypsies, with second-hand clothes and bric-à-brac for sale, and peasant farmers who set up *ad hoc* stalls in the streets around the entrance to the market selling anything from a rabbit or a chicken to bunches of herbs or jars of honey.

Four of the best produce markets are:

Lagos
On two floors, with a fascinating array of fish on the ground floor and fruit and vegetables above.
✉ **Rua das Portas de Portugal**
🕐 Mon–Sat 8–1

Loulé
Set in a striking, tiled, Moorish-style building, dating from the 1930s, and with the most varied range of stalls of any market in the Algarve.
✉ **Praça da República**
🕐 Mon–Sat 8–1

Olhão
The biggest and best in the region – two adjacent halls built in Moorish style, with fish and shellfish for sale in one and fruit and vegetables in the other.
✉ **Avenida 5 de Outubro**
🕐 Mon–Sat 8–1

Silves
Everything for sale under one roof, including delicious bread baked in a wood-fired oven.
✉ **Rua J Estevão**
🕐 Mon–Sat 8–1

Street Markets
Itinerant merchants travel from town to town setting up stalls at what are sometimes called 'gypsy markets' or 'country markets'. In addition, some towns have a 'Saturday market', which centres around the covered market, but which attracts many additional stallholders in the surrounding streets. The stalls sell literally everything you could ever want, from livestock and agricultural machinery to antiques and locally produced ceramics, wicker baskets and lace, clothing, linen and music cassettes.

Main markets:
Albufeira: 1st and 3rd Tuesday of the month (in Orada to the west of the town).
Almancil: 4th Sunday of the month.
Alvor: 2nd Tuesday of the month.
Lagos: 1st Saturday of the month Quarteira: every Wednesday.
Loulé: every Saturday
Monchique: 2nd Friday of the month.

Portimão: 1st Monday of the month (next to the railway station).

Sagres: 1st Friday of the month (opposite the post office).

Silves, Tavira: 3rd Monday of the month.

Antiques

Western Algarve

Lagos
Casa do Papagaio
You cannot miss this shop as you walk down Rua 25 de Abril because of its live parrot, prominently positioned outside the door to catch the attention of passers-by. Inside, the tiny, cramped store is packed with everything from junk to genuine antique statuary.
✉ **Rua 25 de Abril**
🕐 **Mon–Fri 10–1, 3–7, Sat 10–1**

Western Central Algarve

Silves
Antiques Gallery
Up-market antiques store in the square west of the cathedral selling ceramics, glass, jewellery, paintings and fine furniture.
✉ **Largo D J Osório**
🕐 **Mon–Sun 10–8**

Eastern Central Algarve

Faro
Vila Adentro Galleria
Six rooms full of antiques in the old town just north of the cathedral. Everything from inexpensive books, bottles, plates and postcards to medieval religious statuary and paintings.
✉ **Rua do Castelo 21**
🕐 **Mon–Sun 10–8**

Artesanato

Artesanato shops specialise in typical Portuguese products. These include dolls made from hessian, woven baskets, cork products, place mats, coasters and floor mats, lace products such as tablecloths, decorative collars and pillow slips, woollen shawls and chunky sweaters, handmade rugs, brightly painted earthenware jars, copper lamps, almond confectionery, painted cockerels and models of traditional sailing vessels, called caravels, carved in wood. Many also sell ceramics – hand-painted plates, tiles and jugs – though it is more interesting to shop for these at the workshops where they are produced (► Ceramics 107–9).

Western Algarve

Lagos
Helder Castanho
Sells replicas of sailing boats that are destined to become collector's items, using recycled materials.
✉ **Rua Conselheiro Joaquim Machado** ☎ **082 767580**
🕐 **Mon–Sat 8–1, 3–7**

João Calado
Good range of crafts, including iron candelabras, cork products and terracotta jars.
✉ **Torre, near Lagos, on the EN 124** 🕐 **Mon–Sun 8–1, 3–7**

Western Central Algarve

Alvor
Caleidoscopio
An unusual and attractive range of cork products, including handbags and watch straps.
✉ **Rua 25 de Abril 6**
🕐 **Mon–Sat 8–1, 3–7**

Monchique
Casa da Praça
Sells a wide range of handicrafts at reasonable prices.
✉ **Praça Alexandre Herculano**
🕐 **Mon–Sun 8–1, 3–7**

Wines and Spirits
Just head for any supermarket in the Algarve to find a comprehensive stock of local products. Most local wines are best drunk in the Algarve, but one or two travel well: look for the names Barraida or Lagoa on the label. You might also like to buy classic Portuguese wines from beyond the Algarve, such as Dão, *vinho verde* or port. Local liqueurs include distilled arbutus berries (*medronho*) and *amêndoa amarga*, a delicious almond-based liqueur.

Shop Opening Hours

Shops in the Algarve are generally open from Monday to Friday 9–1 and 3–7, and on Saturday 9–1. During the summer, many stay open through the siesta period, especially those in tourist resorts, and until 10PM at night or later. Supermarkets in resorts open on Sundays and holidays. During the winter, opening hours are less predictable. Some shops catering exclusively for tourists close altogether from the beginning of November through to Easter.

Casa do Forno

Traditional souvenirs and crafts.

✉ Rua Dr Francisco Gomes do Avelar ⏱ Mon–Sun 10–1, 3–8

O Descansa Pernas

Cork, pottery, leather goods and ornaments.

✉ Estrada de Saboia ⏱ Mon–Sun 10–1, 3–8

O Poço

Cork products and hand-painted pottery.

✉ Estrada da Fóia ⏱ Mon–Sun 10–1, 3–8

Porches

Arisol

Try this shop whilst visiting the nearby potteries (► Ceramics 107–9).

✉ Alporchinhos, on the EN 125 ⏱ Mon–Sat 8–1, 3–7. Closed Sun

Portimão

José Eliseu

Watch this artist creating products in stained glass.

✉ Vivenda Três Nações, Aldeia das Sobreiras ☎ 082 422364 to arrange a visit

O Aquário

Glass, ceramics, wicker and dolls, plus more up-market Atlantis Crystal glass and Vista Alegre porcelain.

✉ Praça da República ⏱ Mon–Sat 9:30–7 in summer; Mon–Fri 9:30–1, 3–7; Sat 9:30–1 in winter

Silves

Coisas Loiças

Ceramics and handicrafts.

✉ Rua 25 de Abril ⏱ Mon–Sun 10–1, 3–8

Estabelecimento D Sancho

Viennese-style coffee house with large souvenir shop selling ceramics and textiles, next to the entrance to the castle.

✉ Largo do Castelo ⏱ Mon–Sun 10–8

Eastern Central Algarve

Almancil

Al Quatro

Stocks most examples of Algarvian craft.

✉ Estrada de Vale do Lobo ⏱ Mon–Fri 10–1, 2–7

Alte

Café Regional

Café that doubles as a shop selling attractive hand-painted plates and basketry.

✉ Just south of the parish church, in Alte's main square ⏱ Mon–Sun 8–1, 3–7

Galerias Ivette

Painted plates and realistic silk flowers are among the best buys in a huge shop full of every kind of souvenir.

✉ Just southeast of the parish church, in Alte's main square ⏱ Mon–Sun 8–1, 3–7

Faro

Galeria Daquiem Diante

Pottery made into attractive table lamps, colourful rugs and terracotta jars.

✉ Rua do Repouso 6–8 ⏱ Mon–Sun 10–8

Porta da Moura

In the old town, just east of the cathedral square. Full of ceramics, textiles and toys.

✉ Rua do Repouso 5 ⏱ Mon–Sun 10–8

Loulé

Centro de Artesanato

Perhaps the best and most comprehensive display in the Algarve: more unusual items include homemade rugs, ceramics, straw dolls, cork place mats, ornaments made from woven palm leaves, lace shawls, and wood caravels.

✉ **Rua da Barbacã**
🕐 Mon–Sun 8–1, 3–7

O Arco

Adjacent to an arch in the old town walls, selling hand-painted plates with sunflower and fruit motifs.

✉ **Rua das Almadas**
🕐 Mon–Sun 8–1, 3–7

Eastern Algarve

Monte Gordo
Carvela

Candles, mugs, and a range of local pottery.

✉ **Avenida Infante Dom Henrique** 🕐 Mon–Fri 10–1, 3–7, Sat 10–1

Casa Caravela

Specialises in glass and crystal.

✉ **Rua Dr Teófilo Braga**
🕐 Mon–Fri 10–1, 3–7, Sat 10–1

Tavira
Alart

Good range of modern designs in pottery and crafts.

✉ **Rua de Caleria** 🕐
Mon–Fri 10–1, 3–7, Sat 10–1

Porta de Reixa

Central shop with wide-ranging stock.

✉ **Praça da República**
🕐 Mon–Fri 10–1, 3–7, Sat 10–1

Vila Real de Santo António
Estabelecimentos Sol Dourado

Huge product range, including textiles.

✉ **Rua Dr Teófilo Braga**
🕐 Mon–Fri 10–1, 3–8, Sat 10–1

Basketry

Tavira
Artesanato Regional Bazar Tanger

Basket weavers can sometimes be seen at work here making bags, hats, toys, dolls, table mats and floor coverings.

✉ **Rua José Pires Padhina**
🕐 Mon–Sat 10–1, 3–7. Closed Sun

Ceramics and Pottery

Western Algarve

Lagos
O Caixote

A wide range of traditional pottery, including replica chimneypots, mugs and painted plates.

✉ **Rua 25 de Abril**
🕐 Mon–Sat 8–1, 3–7

Western Central Algarve

Alvor
Artesanato Alexandre

Painted pottery and other souvenirs.

✉ **Rua Dr António José de Almeida** 🕐 Mon–Sat 8–1, 3–7

Porches
Artesanato Reis

One of several huge pottery works on the EN 125, unmissable because of the advertising signs and yards stacked high with pottery of every shape, size and colour. Visitors can watch craftsmen at work painting colourful motifs depicting flowers, fish and birds.

✉ **Porches, beside the EN 125**
☎ 082 381668 🕐 Mon–Sat 9–8 (to 6 in winter). Closed Sun

The Cockerel of Barcelos

Souvenir shops throughout Portugal sell cockerels of all sizes, in many different colours and guises, and the Algarve is no exception. This national symbol stands for honesty and truthfulness. According to a popular folk story, the guest at a banquet in Barcelos was publicly accused of theft. Hauled before a judge, he was pronounced guilty and sentenced to hang. To prove his innocence, the condemned man pointed to a cockerel that was being served to the judge on a silver plate platter and declared that the bird would crow. To everyone's astonishment the bird stood up and duly crowed.

Basketry

Baskets make lightweight and inexpensive presents. Made all over the Algarve, and sold in *artesanato* shops, the capacious bags are derived from the sort that peasant farmers have developed over the centuries for carrying produce to and from the fields and markets – flexible shoulder bags and panniers made from straw or *esparto* grass.

Portimão
Domingos de Jesus Filipe
Large range of traditional products.

⊠ Penina, by the EN 125
🕓 Mon–Sun 10–8

Eastern Central Algarve

Albufeira
Infante Dom Henrique
Specialises in fine earthenware.

⊠ Rua Cândido dos Reis
🕓 Mon–Sun 10–8

Loulé
Alegrete
Here you will find terracotta jars, garden ornaments and wood-fired cooking pots with an attractive patina.

⊠ Rua Miguel Bombarda 66–8
🕓 Mon–Sun 8–1, 3–7

Casa Louart
Hand-painted pottery in bold designs.

⊠ Rua Dom Paio Peres
🕓 Mon–Sun 8–1, 3–7

Liliana Domingos
Good selection of more unusual hand-painted pottery.

⊠ Rua das Bicas Velhas
🕓 Mon–Sun 8–1, 3–7

Eastern Algarve

Tavira
Artesanato Regional Casa Matias
Traditional pottery based in the market.

⊠ Mercado Municipal, Rua do Cais 🕓 Mon–Sat 10–1, 3–7. **Closed Sun**

Leatherware

Portuguese craftsmanship in leather is renowned throughout Europe. The Algarve has a number of shops selling beautifully made goods at good-value prices.

Algarvian leather workers also specialise in tooled leather, and there is a long tradition of saddle-making in the region.

Western Central Algarve

Portimão
Chic Shoes
This shop specialises in handmade leather boots and shoes.

⊠ Rua Direita 🕓 Mon–Sat 10–1, 3–8

Leather Factory
The Leather Factory sells everything from shoes and belts to skirts and waistcoats.

⊠ Rua Dr J V Mealha
🕓 Mon–Sat 10–1, 3–8

Eastern Central Algarve

Faro
Oberon
Smart shoes, handbags and a range of accessories.

⊠ Rua de Santo António 67
🕓 Mon–Sun 10–8

Loulé
Correaria Moderna
Watch saddles and harnesses being made and shop for leather belts, wallets, purses and handbags.

⊠ Rua da Barbacã
🕓 Mon–Sat 8–1, 3–7

Malas Vinhas
The leather goods on sale here include sandals, boots and handbags.

✉ Rua 5 de Outubro 55
🕐 Mon–Sat 8–1, 3–7.
Closed Sun

Metalwork

Loulé
Barracha
Cataplanas and cooking pots, reproduction stills, lighting and fireside ornaments in copper, wrought iron and brass.
✉ Rua José Fernando Guerreiro (to the south of the market) 🕐 Mon–Sat 8–1, 3-7.
Closed Sun

Caldeiraria Louletana
Workshop specialising in handmade brass and copper goods, which you can watch being made.
✉ Rua da Barbacã
🕐 Mon–Sat 8–1, 3–7.
Closed Sun

Miscellaneous

Eastern Central Algarve

Albufeira
Pro Disc
Carries a huge selection of *fado* music and Portuguese folk on tape and CD.
✉ Areias de São João
🕐 Mon–Sun 10–1, 3–8

Almancil
Florida Golf
Everything for the golf fanatic.
✉ Rua 5 de Outubro
🕐 Mon–Sat 8–1, 3–7

Griffin Bookshop
The Algarve's best-stocked English-language bookshop with a good range of fiction and non-fiction titles for children and adults, plus second-hand books.

✉ Rua 5 de Outubro 206-A
☎ 089 393904 🕐 Mon–Sat 8–1, 3–7

Faro
António Zucannel
Designer fashions for women: Versace, Polo, etc.
✉ Rua de Santo António 48
🕐 Mon–Fri 10–1, 3–7, Sat 10–1

Galerias Santo António
Small shopping centre with various shops selling books, footwear, souvenirs, jewellery and fashions.
✉ Rua de Santo António 25
🕐 Mon–Fri 10–1, 3–7, Sat 10–1

Palloram
Up-market men's fashions.
✉ Rua de Santo António 53
🕐 Mon–Fri 10–1, 3–7, Sat 10–1

Eastern Algarve

Olhão
A Margerida
Lace, silk flowers, picture frames.
✉ Rua do Comércio
🕐 Mon–Fri 10–1, 3–7, Sat 10–1

A Roldana
Reproductions of rustic country-style furniture, table lamps made from natural and glazed terracotta, handmade paper shades.
✉ Rua Miguel Bombarda
🕐 Mon–Fri 10–1, 3–7, Sat 10–1

Tavira
Kawé Artesanato Africano
Art from Portugal's former African colonies, including masks, drums and elongated figures carved in wood.
✉ Rua Dr António Cabrera 18–20 🕐 Mon–Fri 10–1, 3–7, Sat 10–1

Algarvian Pottery
Ceramic techniques were introduced to the Algarve by the Moors and the tradition has never died. Among the region's products are terracotta pots for use in the garden, and hand-painted jugs, plates and bowls, decorated with brightly coloured fruit and flower motifs. Also popular are hand-painted cockerels (*gallos*) in every size and shape, and miniature versions of the ornate Algarvian chimneys that are seen on older houses throughout the region. In addition, *azulejos* are still made – thick, chunky irregular tiles with blue and white or polychrome painted decorations. Genuine antique *azulejos* are sold singly and are expensive, but modern tiles are sold in sets for use as floor or wall decorations.

Children's Attractions

Watersports

Think twice before allowing your children to ride on water inflatables, such as ringos and bananas, which are pulled along at high speed behind a powerboat. Though popular and heavily promoted, the bumpy ride has caused a number of injuries, and nervous children are easily frightened. Stick with the more sedate pedalos instead.

Theme Parks and Water Parks

The Algarve has four large water parks, and although half-day tickets are available, it is easy and enjoyable to make them the focus of a whole day. Facilities are graded so that children of all ages will find something to thrill and challenge them, from junior slides and pools for younger children to 'corkscrew slides' and 'black holes' for the older ones. Fully qualified lifeguards are on hand to ensure safety, and there are snack bars and restaurants for refreshment.

Carvoeiro
The Big One

Exciting attractions, with names like 'Raging Rapids', 'Flying Carpets' and 'Crazy Leap', make this a must for the daring.

✉ **On the EN 125 main highway at Alcantarilha** ☎ **082 322827** Ⓒ **Daily 10–6. Closed Nov–Easter**

Zoomarine

One ticket provides entry to a number of attractions, including the marine zoo and the water park. Shows featuring dolphins, seals and parrots are staged throughout the day, and the other attractions include an aquarium, sea museum, cinema, funfair, swimming pools with slides and whirlpools, and restaurants.

✉ **On the EN 125 at the Guia junction, near Albufeira** ☎ **089 561104** Ⓒ **Daily 10–6. Closed Nov–Easter**

Quarteira
Atlantic Park

Thrilling slides for the energetic guaranteed, with lots of long water slides and tunnels.

✉ **On the EN 125 at Quatro Estradas, near Quarteira** ☎ **089 397282** Ⓒ **Daily 9–6. Closed Nov–Easter**

Slide and Splash

Experience the exciting 'Black Hole' whirlpool at this popular park. Facilities include shops, bars and a restaurant. Slide and Splash runs buses during the summer, collecting customers from pick-up points in the main coastal resorts.

✉ **On the EN 125 at Vale de Deus, at Estômbar, near Armação de Pêra** ☎ **082 341685** Ⓒ **Daily 10–6. Closed Nov–Easter**

Mini-golf

Albufeira
Krazy Golf

This fun course, bigger than most of its kind, is set in grounds planted with tropical palms among ponds and lakes. Visit llamas and goats in the animal farm, or try your hand at riding a water-scooter on one of the lakes. There is also a quad-bike racing circuit. If the noise gets too much, head for the bar or pizzeria and let the children get on with it.

✉ **Signposted on the EN 125 at the Guia junction, near Algoz** ☎ **082 574134** Ⓒ **Jun–Sep daily 9:30–11, Oct –May daily 9:30–7**

Trains, Boat Trips and Jeep Safaris

The Algarve railway runs from Vila Real de Santo António to Lagos, travelling at a sedate speed. Children will enjoy a return ride, especially as the line passes through some interesting coastal scenery. In Praia da Rocha, the Rocha Express road train runs along the 2km promenade in summer, leaving Miradouro at half-hourly intervals from 10–12:30 and 3–6:30, calling at Fortaleza, Praia do Vau and Rotunda Presidente. Buy your tickets on board.

Albufeira
Zebra Safari
This jeep safari (suitable for teenagers) involves exploring some of the lesser-known parts of the Algarve, travelling along unsurfaced roads in zebra-striped jeeps. Also adventure days and treasure hunts, canoeing, mountain biking and hiking expeditions.
✉ The Strip ☎ 089 586360
🕐 Daily 10–1, 3–7

Lagos
Aquabus
A 'yellow submarine' – a boat with huge windows in the hull, designed to let you see the marine life beneath the sea without having to don wet suit and snorkel.
✉ The Marina, Avenida dos Descobrimentos ☎ 082 767794
🕐 Sailings depart at regular intervals daily from 9AM to 10PM

Watersports
The Watersports Centre at Meia Praia, near Lagos, runs special 'Kids' Days' aimed at children aged from 9 to 16. They learn to windsurf or improve their existing skills, as well as swim and play volleyball in the care of trainers and lifeguards.
✉ Meia Praia Beach, Lagos ☎ 0931 830591 🕐 Jun–Sep Mon–Fri 10:30–4

Horse Riding
The Algarve has numerous stables offering riding lessons for everyone from adults to infants and from total beginners to seasoned hackers, usually with English-speaking instructors. Lessons can be booked by the hour, or you can go trekking through glorious countryside or cantering along the beach on half- or full-day trips.

Since most of the stables are based in the countryside, they will send transport to meet you, and will provide picnic food or refreshments for longer outings.

Vale Navio
✉ Albufeira
☎ 089 542870

Horses' Paradise
✉ Almancil ☎ 089 394189

Casa Galaraz Riding Centre
✉ Benagil/Carvoeiro
☎ 082 358055

Centro Hipico, Quinta da Atalia
✉ Lagos ☎ 082 761921

Tiffany's Riding Centre
✉ Lagos
☎ 082 96444

Grande Val de Ferro Riding
✉ Mexilhoeira
☎ 082 968444

Centro Hipico da Penina
✉ Portimão
☎ 082 415415

Paraíso dos Cavalos
✉ Vale do Lobo
☎ 089 394189

Centro Hipico
✉ Vilamoura
☎ 089 322675

Indulgence
Fair-haired children may get fed up of being patted on the head or shoulders by strangers, but it is a fact of life that the Portuguese regard them as especially fortunate, so any would-be lottery-prize winner will want a bit of your child's luck. No harm is meant – the Portuguese love children. In restaurants, children are welcomed and indulged, and parents can bask in the extra attention that well-behaved families get wherever they go.

Fado & Cinemas

Film Festival

Film buffs may be interested in the Algarve's International Film Festival in May, when Portuguese and foreign films are shown at cinemas in Alvor, Lagoa, Lagos and Loulé, in their original language; ☎ 01 851 3615 for further details.

Casino

There is a casino in Praia da Rocha's 5-star Hotel Algarve, with free entry to the ground floor where there are slot machines and video games, and no dress code. Passports must be shown as proof of age to gain access to the gaming tables, and there is a small entry charge; visitors must be smartly dressed in jacket and tie. The nightly dinner and floor show starts at 8:30 (☎ 082 415001 for further information).

Fado

Fado is unique to Portugal; like the blues, it is claimed to have its origins in African slave music, but the music developed its present form in mid-19th-century Lisbon. *Fado* means 'fate', and the lyrics of each three-minute song express the sadness and yearning occasioned by lost or unrequited love or the vicissitudes of life.

The *fadista*, or singer, traditionally wears black. The accompaniment is provided by two musicians, one of whom plays the pear-shaped *quitarra portuguesa* (a 12-stringed Portuguese guitar), while the other provides the bass line on a Spanish guitar.

Western Algarve

Lagos
Restaurante A Muralha
✉ 15 Rua da Atalaia ☎ 082 763659 🎵 Nightly performances. Closed Mon

Western Central Algarve

Alvor
Hotel Delphim
Holds *fado* evenings one week, folk evenings the next.
✉ Praia dos Três Irmãos
☎ 082 458901

Lagoa
Restaurante Casa Velha
✉ 62-r/c Mouz Albuq ☎ 082 342600 🎵 Performances Sat at 9PM

Porches
Restaurante Porches Velho
✉ EN 125 main highway at Porches, near Lagoa ☎ 082 381692 🎵 Performances Fri and Sat at 9PM

Portimão
Restaurante A Vela
✉ 97-r/c Dr Manuel Alma
☎ 082 414016
🎵 Performances Thu and Sat

Silves
Quinta Pomona
✉ 26-r/c 5 Outubro ☎ 082 416350 🎵 Performances Wed and Thu 8PM

Eastern Central Algarve

Albufeira
Bar Jardim d'Allah
✉ Beco José B Sousa ☎ 089 586362 🎵 Performances Thu at 10PM

Restaurante Casa Velha
✉ Casa Leão, Santa Eulalia
☎ 089 541926
🎵 Performances Fri

Vale do Lobo
Le Meridien Dona Filipe Hotel
✉ Vale do Lobo, 8136 Almancil ☎ 089 394141 🎵 *Fado* performances Mon, folk song and dance Wed

Cinemas

Films are shown in their original language, usually English.

Faro
Cinema Santo António
✉ Rua Dr Francisco Gomes
☎ 089 823308 🎵 Daily 9:30

Loulé
Cinema Charlot
✉ Avenida 25 Abril ☎ 089 416405

Praia da Rocha
Cinema da Rocha
✉ Praia da Rocha ☎ 082 419081 🎵 Daily 3:30, 6:30, 9:30, Fri and Sat midnight

Boat Trips, Fishing & Watersports

Boat Trips and Fishing

Western Algarve

Lagos
Bom Dia
The Bom Dia company specialises in trips to explore the marine caves of the nearby coastline. Visitors travel along the coast in a tall-masted sailing ship, using smaller boats to explore the marine grottoes.
✉ **Lagos marina** ☎ **082 764670**

Bluewater Sportsfishing
Daily big-game fishing trips.
✉ **Lagos marina** ☎ **082 768246**

Sagres
Coastal tours
Explore the awe-inspiring cliffs of World's End and the windswept Costa Vicentina on a two-hour excursion that departs daily at 2PM. Three-hour fishing trips for first-timers and experienced anglers, departing daily at 4:30PM, offer the chance to hook squid, sea bass, bream and mackerel. If you want bigger challenges, shark-fishing trips depart at 8AM Tuesday and Thursday (half-day excursions) and Saturday (full day).
✉ **Turinfo, Praça de Republica** ☎ **082 64520**

Western Central Algarve

Portimão
Arade River Cruises
If you are prone to sea-sickness and do not relish the idea of a boat trip on a potentially rough sea, try cruising up the more gentle Arade River instead, from its estuary at Portimão to the Moorish castle town of Silves. The same company organises trips to explore the marine caves of Carvoeiro, Benagil and Praia da Marinha and the cliffs at Algar Seco.
✉ **Leãozinho Arade River Cruises, Portimão harbour** ☎ **082 415156**

Cepemar
Big-game fishing for hammerhead shark, marlin, swordfish and bonito. Beginners welcome.
✉ **Rua António Dias Cordeiro 1** ☎ **082 425341**

Watersports

Western Algarve

Praia da Luz
Watersports School
Windsurfing, sailing, water-skiing and boat trips are all available.
✉ **Praia da Luz harbour** ☎ **082 778581**

Sea Sports Centre
Fully-licensed diving school where you can hire equipment or join courses designed for beginners and advanced divers. Look out for details of occasional night dives and wreck-exploring trips.
✉ **Avenida dos Pescadores, Loja 4** ☎ **082 789538**

Eastern Central Algarve

Albufeira
Atlantic Diving
This PADI-affiliated British sub-aqua club organises courses for novices, sports divers and experts.
✉ **Praia de Aveiro** ☎ **089 587479**

Flying
If you want to get above the waves rather than on or beneath them, try one of the parascending cruises that depart at 10, 12, 4 and 6 daily from the marina at Vilamoura. The parachutes are controlled by a hydraulic winch which guarantees a gentle take-off and landing – ideal for first-timers (Marina Watersports, ☎ 089 388149 for further details).

Keeping Fit

Jeep Safaris
Many travel agents in the Algarve advertise jeep safaris, which explore the unmetalled roads of the Algarvian interior around Monchique, or hidden and inaccessible coves along the west-facing Atlantic coast. One of the more environmentally aware companies is Zebra Safari, based in Albufeira, which organises daily jeep safaris, but also has trekking, birdwatching, ecological tours and horse safaris on its programme (☎ 089 586360).

Western Algarve

Burgau
Burgau Sports Centre
Tennis and squash courts, aerobics sessions, sauna, gymnasium, pool, table tennis, swimming pool and children's playground. Coaching available.
✉ Burgau ☎ 082 697350

Praia da Luz
The facilities at the Luz Bay and Ocean clubs are open to non-residents and include swimming pools, saunas, a Turkish bath, gym, mini-golf, tennis and squash courts.
✉ Avenida Pescadores, Praia da Luz, 8600 Lagos ☎ 082 789472

Western Central Algarve

Carvoeiro
The Rocha Brava Tennis Club is open to visitors, who are encouraged to use the facilities and join in tournaments. Equipment hire and coaches available.
✉ Rocha Brava, Praia do Carvoeiro ☎ 082 358856

Eastern Central Algarve

Vale do Lobo
Barringtons
Apart from the well-known golf academy, with its floodlit driving range and instruction, this complex includes squash courts, a cricket pitch with nets, a fitness centre, sauna, Turkish bath and jacuzzi, indoor and outdoor swimming pools and a snooker room.
✉ Vale do Lobo ☎ 089 396622

David Lloyd Club
The David Lloyd Club, owned by the former British international, is well known amongst tennis circles and the 12-court complex is used as the basis for coaching and tournament matches.
✉ Vale do Lobo ☎ 089 396926

Desportos Aquáticos
Mountain-bike excursions through the Ria Formosa reserve.
✉ Quinta do Lago ☎ 089 394929

Vilamoura
Rock Garden
This is one of the Algarve's best-equipped sports centres, offering indoor and outdoor swimming pools, tennis and squash courts. Also available are a Turkish bath, snooker tables, table tennis, darts, a gym and a fitness suite.
✉ Aldeia do Campo ☎ 089 322740

Vilamoura Tennis Centre
The Vilamoura Tennis Club, just off the marina, has 12 courts and a restaurant and bar. Equipment hire and individual or group tuition available.
✉ Vilamoura ☎ 089 302369

Eastern Algarve

Tavira
Rent a Bike
Explore Tavira and Ria Formosa Reserve by mountain bike; four-hour cycle tours are available, departing Monday at 9AM and Friday at 2:30PM.
✉ Rua do Forno 22 ☎ 081 321973

Golf

The Algarve is one of Europe's most popular destinations for golfing holidays, with many specialist tour operators. Large numbers of visitors come here for no other reason than to spend a week perfecting their skills. The region has 16 courses, and some of them are renowned throughout the world for their challenging terrain and beautiful natural surroundings. The following courses are among those highly rated by golfers:

Western Central Algarve

Alvor
Alto Golf
This cliff-top course enjoys superb views of the sea and the Serra de Monchique mountains. Designed by Sir Henry Cotton, the challenging course is famous for its 16th hole, one of the longest in Europe. Golf school with practice bunker and putting green. 18 holes, par 72.
✉ **Quinta do Alto do Poço, Alvor** ☎ **082 416913**

Carvoeiro
Vale de Milho
Nine-hole par-27 course with challenging water hazards.
✉ **Apartado 273, Carvoeiro** ☎ **082 358502**

Vale da Pinta
New 18-hole course, built around an ancient olive grove.
✉ **Carvoeiro** ☎ **082 340900**

Pestana Golf
The base for the David Leadbetter Golf Academy, with two scenic, 18-hole courses.
✉ **Carvoeiro** ☎ **082 340900**

Eastern Central Algarve

Vale do Lobo
Quinta do Lago
Designed by Henry Cotton, the two 18-hole, par-72 courses feature lakes and challenging bunkers. Rated one of the best golf complexes in Europe, the Portuguese Open and other international tournaments are regularly hosted here.
✉ **Quinta do Lago** ☎ **089 396141**

Pinheiros Altos
This par-72, 18-hole course begins in attractive pine woods, while the back nine holes run alongside the Ria Formosa Nature Reserve.
✉ **Quinta do Lago** ☎ **089 396141**

San Lorenzo
To play this 27-hole course (with three 9-hole loops) you must be a guest at the luxurious Dona Filipa or Penina hotels. Keen golfers consider the expense worthwhile for the chance to play a course that is currently rated number 2 in Europe, with its famous 7th hole (on the yellow loop) straddling two ravines.
✉ **Quinta do Lago** ☎ **089 396522**

Vilamoura
The Vilamoura estate, west of Faro, has three courses designed for a range of abilities, from the testing Vilamoura I to the 27-hole Vilamoura III course with three 9-hole combinations, set among lakes.
✉ **Vilamoura** ☎ **Old Course 089 322650; Pinhal 089 321562; Laguna 089 380722**

Helicopter Flights
If you want to celebrate a victory on the golf course, you can splash out on a 15-minute helicopter flight for a bird's-eye view of the barrier islands and lagoons around Faro (details from Globalterra, Almancil, (☎ 089 396881). For a less expensive view from the air, try microlighting from the Algarve Airports Centre, near Lagos (for details of lessons and flights ☎ 082 762906).

What's on When

Information

Pick up *Algarve Events* from the airport as you arrive or from tourist information centres. The brochure lists forthcoming cultural events in the region for the month ahead.

February

Carnival (weekend preceding Shrove Tuesday): steel barriers go up all over the Algarve on the Saturday before Shrove Tuesday, sealing off town centres from traffic so that the weekend's carnival can proceed without interruption. Typically, Saturday sees local children take part in a costume parade through the streets, while the irreverent 'satirical parade' takes place the following day. Loulé Carnival has the biggest and best procession, with colourful floats, bands and scantily clad dancers. Be warned, though, that water bombs, eggs, flour and other substances are hurled at spectators during this and other carnival parades, so don't wear your best clothes.

April

Holy Week (especially Palm Sunday, Good Friday and Easter Saturday): religious processions in the streets of many towns, when actors re-enact scenes from the Passion and Crucifixion of Christ.

May

May Day Folk Festival (1): traditional singing and folk dancing, with food and drink on sale in Alcoutim, Albufeira, Alte and Monchique.

June/July

International Music Festival: sponsored by the Gulbenkian Foundation, this is the biggest arts festival in the Algarve, with top international artists performing in a number of centres, including Albufeira and Silves.

July

Tavira Jazz Festival (all month): local and international musicians come together for this celebration.
Alcoutim Handicraft Festival (2nd or 3rd week): see the best of the region's crafts as stalls line the streets.
Silves Beer Festival (all month): Silves Castle is taken over by brass bands and folk dancers in this celebration of Portuguese and international beers.
Feira do Carmo: Faro's own handicraft festival.

August

Fatacil (3rd week): Lagoa's country fair is a showcase for local agriculture, industry and commerce, with live bands and food and wine tastings.
Summer in Tavira: fado, folk and classical music, plus folk dancing in the open air in the city's parks and gardens.
Fish Festival (11 Aug): Cabanas celebrates the fruits of the sea with a market, folk music and dancing, and *fado* music.
Banho de 29 (29 Aug): fireworks and live music to celebrate the end of the holiday season in Lagos.

September

National Folklore Festival (1st week): Portuguese folk music and dancing troupes come from as far away as Brazil and Madeira.
Lagoa Wine Festival (2nd week): tastings to promote local vintages.
Nossa Senhora das Dores (3rd week): country fair food stalls, fairground attractions and folk concerts, starting in Monte Gordo and moving on to Tavira.

Practical Matters

Above: *Ponta da Piedade*
Right: *traditional costume
provides sun protection*

TIME DIFFERENCES

GMT	Portugal	Germany	USA (NY)	Netherlands	Spain
12 noon	12 noon	→1PM	←7AM	→1PM	→1PM

BEFORE YOU GO

WHAT YOU NEED

● Required ○ Suggested ▲ Not required	UK	Germany	USA	Netherlands	Spain
Passport/National Identity Card	●	●	●	●	●
Visa	▲	▲	▲	▲	▲
Onward or Return Ticket	○	○	○	○	○
Health Inoculations	▲	▲	▲	▲	▲
Health Documentation (reciprocal agreement document, ➤ 123, Health)	▲	▲	▲	▲	▲
Travel Insurance	○	○	○	○	○
Driving Licence (National)	●	●	●	●	●
Car Insurance Certificate (if own car)	●	●	●	●	●
Car registration document (if own car)	●	●	●	●	●

WHEN TO GO

Faro

■ High season

□ Low season

15°C	16°C	18°C	21°C	24°C	30°C	35°C	37°C	33°C	28°C	19°C	17°C
JAN	FEB	MAR	APR	MAY	JUN	JUL	AUG	SEP	OCT	NOV	DEC

 Sun   Sunshine & showers

TOURIST OFFICES

In the UK
Portuguese National
Tourist Office
22–25A Sackville Street
London W1X 1DE
☎ 0171 494 1441
Fax: 0171 494 1868

In the USA
Portuguese National
Tourist Office
590 5th Avenue, 4th Floor
New York
NY 10036
☎ 212/354 4403
Fax: 212/764 6137

POLICE 112

FIRE 112

AMBULANCE 112

WHEN YOU ARE THERE

ARRIVING

It is possible to drive to the Algarve from all parts of continental Europe, but most visitors arrive by air. Faro airport is served by flights from most European airports, by means of scheduled and charter flights. Because of the region's popularity as a winter destination, seats on direct flights get booked up well in advance and you might have to fly via Lisbon and drive. TAP Air Portugal is the national airline (in Faro ☎ 0808 213141)

Faro Airport	**Journey times**
Kilometres to city centre	
	N/A
●━━━━━━━━━●	🚌 15 minutes
4 kilometres	🚗 10 minutes

MONEY

Portuguese currency is divided into *escudos* and *centavos*. A dollar sign denotes the currency, written after the *escudos* amount to avoid confusion with the US dollar (eg 230$50 means 230 *escudos* and 50 *centavos*). The coins in circulation are 200, 100, 50, 20, 10, 5 and 2.5 *escudos* (rare); notes are in denominations of 10,000, 5,000, 2,000, 1,000 and 500 *escudos*. MasterCard, Visa, American Express and Diners Club cards are widely accepted, as are travellers' cheques. On 1 January 1999 the euro became the official currency of Portugal and the *escudo* became a denomination of the euro. *Escudo* notes continue to be legal tender during a transitional period. Euro banknotes and coins are likely to be introduced by 1 January 2002.

TIME

 The Algarve observes Greenwich Mean Time during the winter months; during the summer, from late March to late September, the time is GMT plus one hour.

CUSTOMS

 YES

Goods Obtained Duty Free Inside the EU or Goods Bought Outside the EU (Limits)
Alcohol (over 22%vol): 1L *or*
Alcohol (not over 22%vol): 2L *and*
Still table wine: 2L
Cigarettes: 200 *or* Cigars: 50 *or* Tobacco: 250gms
Perfume: 60ml
Toilet water: 250ml
Goods Bought Duty and Tax Paid for Own Use Inside the EU (Guidance Levels):
Alcohol (over 22%vol): 10L
Alcohol (not over 22%vol): 20L *and* Wine (max 60L sparkling), 90L, Beer (110L), Cigarettes: 800; Cigars: 200; Tobacco: 1kg
Perfume and Toilet Water: no limit

You must be 17 or over to benefit from alcohol and tobacco allowances.

 NO

Narcotic drugs, firearms, ammunition, offensive weapons, obscene material, unlicensed animals.

EMBASSIES AND CONSULATES

UK 082 417800	**Germany** 089 803148	**USA** 01 727 3300 (Lisbon)	**Netherlands** 089 20903	**Spain** 081 544888

WHEN YOU ARE THERE

TOURIST OFFICES

Algarve Tourism Regional Office
● Avenida 5 de Outubro 18
  8000 Faro
  ☎ 089 800400
  Fax: 089 800489

Local Offices
● Albufeira
  Rua 5 de Outubro 18
  ☎ 089 585279

● Faro
  Rua da Misericórdia 8–12
  ☎ 089 803604

● Lagos
  Largo Marquês de Pombal
  ☎ 082 763031

● Loulé
  Edifício do Castelo
  ☎ 089 463900

● Monchique
  Largo dos Chorões
  ☎ 082 911189

● Monte Gordo
  Avenida Marginal
  ☎ 081 544495

● Olhão
  Largo da Lagoa
  ☎ 089 713936

● Portimão
  Largo 1 de Dezembro
  ☎ 082 419131

● Silves
  Rua 25 de Abril
  ☎ 082 442255

● Tavira
  Rua da Galeria 9
  ☎ 081 322511

NATIONAL HOLIDAYS

J	F	M	A	M	J	J	A	S	O	N	D
1	(2)	(2)	1(2)	1	1(1)		1		1	1	4

1 Jan	New Year
Feb (dates vary)	Shrove Tuesday and Ash Wednesday
Mar/Apr	Good Friday
Mar/Apr	Easter Monday
25 Apr	Day of the Revolution
1 May	Labour Day
Jun (date varies)	Corpus Christi
10 Jun	National Day
15 Aug	Feast of the Assumption
5 Oct	Republic Day
1 Nov	All Saints' Day
1 Dec	Restoration of Independence Day
8 Dec	Feast of the Immaculate Conception
25 Dec	Christmas Day
26 Dec	St Stephen's Day

OPENING HOURS

○ Shops	● Main Post Offices
● Offices	● Museums/Monuments
● Banks	● Pharmacies

8AM 9AM 10AM NOON 1PM 2PM 4PM 5PM 7PM

☐ Day   ☐ Midday
☐ Evening

Shops catering to tourists open all day in the high season, until 9 or 10 in the evening, including Sundays and public holidays.

Larger stores and supermarkets increasingly ignore the lunch break and are open continuously from 9 to 7, with some supermarkets staying open until 10 (5 on Sunday).

Pharmacies open late on a duty rota (posted on pharmacy doors). Times of museum and church opening vary greatly – see individual museums for details.

DRIVE ON THE RIGHT

TOILETS CHARGE

★★
★★

PUBLIC TRANSPORT

 Trains The Algarve railway line follows the south coast from Lagos in the west to Vila Real de Santo António in the east. Although the line is not much more than 130km in length, it can take up to 4½ hours to travel from one end to the other. Stations can be 6km or more from the towns that they serve, so check the map before deciding to use the train. It is cheap, however, and provides views of some fine coastal scenery. Tourist offices have timetables, and tickets should be bought before you get on the train, or else you risk a fine.

 Buses Modern express bus services link most towns in the Algarve. Services are provided by a number of companies. EVA is the biggest, and it sells a useful Passe Turístico (Tourist Pass), which allows unlimited use of the network for three or seven days. Bus routes principally follow the main roads, and so are not a reliable way of exploring the more remote countryside. Up-to-date timetables and route maps are available from tourist offices, and from the bus station (Terminal Rodoviário) in each of the Algarve's main towns.

 Ferries Although most people now travel from Portugal to Spain along the motorway bridge that links the two countries across the Guadiana, ferries do still operate. The car and passenger ferry from Vila Real to Ayamonte departs at 40-minute intervals throughout the day, and fishermen ferry passengers from Alcoutim to San Lúcar on demand. Ferry services also take visitors to the barrier islands in the Ria Formosa Nature Reserve during the summer months, departing from Tavira and Olhão at regular intervals during the day.

CAR RENTAL

 The major car rental firms are represented in the Algarve, as well as several local companies who offer slightly cheaper rates. All rental firms send a courtesy bus to meet you at the airport on arrival, transporting you to their depot on the Faro airport road; alternatively, they will deliver the car to your hotel or villa.

TAXIS

 In towns, it is usual to hire taxis from a rank. They may stop if flagged down, especially in the countryside. Rates for some journeys are fixed. Short journeys across town should be metered. For longer journeys, you can negotiate an hourly rate. Try to find a driver who speaks your language and who has a modern well-maintained car.

DRIVING

 Speed limit on motorways: **120kph**

 Speed limit on main roads: **80kph**

 Speed limit on urban roads: **60 or 40kph**

 It is mandatory for drivers and passengers to wear seat belts as fitted.

 Random breath testing is carried out. Limit: 5ml per litre.

 Petrol (*gasolina*) comes in two grades: lead-free (*sem chumbo*) and 4-star (*super*). Diesel (*gasóleo*) is also available. Most villages and towns have a petrol station, and they are generally open from 8 to 8.

 All the car rental companies in the Algarve run their own breakdown and rescue services, details of which will be given to you when you rent your car. Main highways have orange SOS telephones for use in an emergency. Members of motoring organisations such as the AA and RAC can use the services of the ACP (Automóvel Clube de Portugal) ☎ 089 805753.

PERSONAL SAFETY

Crime in the Algarve is extremely rare. If you are the victim of theft, get help from a hotel or holiday representative because they know the correct procedures and can deal with the bureaucracy. To make an insurance claim you must report thefts to the local police station and get a copy of the written statement.

- Leave your valuables in the hotel safe.
- Don't leave valuables in cars.
- Don't leave unattended valuables on the beach or poolside.
- Beware of pickpockets.

National Police assistance:
☎ **122** from any call box

TELEPHONES

Telephones are found in many cafés, and there are booths in every town or village. Some only take phonecards, for 50 or 120 units, which can be bought from newsagents and cafés. A 50-unit card will give you about 5 minutes' worth of overseas calls. To call the Algarve from abroad, dial 351 (the international code for Portugal), then the area code (82 – Western Algarve, 89 – Central Algarve, 81 – Eastern Algarve). Within the Algarve you only need the five- or six-digit number if you are dialling another number with the same area code: otherwise you need to dial the area code, including the initial 0.

International Dialling Codes	
From the Algarve to:	
UK:	**00 44**
Germany:	**00 49**
USA & Canada:	**00 1**
Netherlands:	**00 31**
Spain:	**00 34**

POST

Post offices (*correios*) are found in main towns. In Faro, the most central post office is on Largo do Carmo, and post restante services are available here, and at all main post offices. Stamps can be bought from newsagents and hotel kiosks. Open: main office Mon–Fri 8:30 or 9–6 , Sat 9–12:30. Smaller offices close from 12:30–2:30.

ELECTRICITY

The power supply in Portugal is: 220 volts AC. Sockets take two-pronged

continental plugs, so an adaptor is needed for non-continental appliances, and a transformer for devices operating on 100–120 volts.

TIPS/GRATUITIES

Yes ✓ No ✗		
Restaurants (service included)	✓	10%
Bar service	✓	small change
Taxis	✓	10%
Tour guides	✗	
Porters	✓	300$
Chambermaids	✗	
Hairdressers	✓	10%
Cloakroom attendants	✓	small change
Toilets	✗	

What to photograph: the Algarve's wild coastline, wind-eroded sandstone cliffs, markets, flowers, traditional costumes, donkey carts and ploughs drawn by horse or mule.
Best time to photograph: the light is best before 10AM; after this the intensity of the sun can bleach out details. Sunsets can be spectacular in the west.
Buying film: most hotels have shops selling film and batteries, and there is usually at least one specialist photo shop in every town, selling film and offering processing services, .

HEALTH

Insurance
Nationals of EU member countries can get medical treatment in the Algarve with the relevant documentation (Form E111 for UK nationals), although it is still advisable to take out travel insurance to cover medical emergencies. Most private clinics and doctors in the Algarve will treat you in your hotel provided you have insurance cover.

Dental Services
Dental services in the Algarve are excellent. Dentists advertise their services in the free English and German-language magazines available from most hotels, and in the monthly publication called *Algarve Living*.

Sun Advice
The sun can be intense in the Algarve at any time of the year, and it is possible to burn with less than an hour's exposure. If you are out walking on cliff-tops or bare hills, it is best to cover vulnerable parts of your body, including your neck, legs and arms.

Drugs
Chemists (*farmâcia*) are open Mon–Fri 9–1 and 3–7, and Sat 9–12:30 . Some open through lunch, and there is a late-night duty rota, posted in pharmacy windows. Take supplies of any drugs that you take regularly, since there is no guarantee that they will be available locally. However, many drugs are available from chemists in Portugal that require prescriptions in other countries. This is partly because pharmacists are skilled paramedics, trained to diagnose a range of problems and sell appropriate medicines.

Safe Water
Tap water is safe to drink, but can be unpleasant to taste because of the minerals it contains. Bottled water is widely available; ask for fizzy water (*água com gás*) or still (*água sem gás*).

CONCESSIONS

Students/Youths Museums have lower rates of admission for students, and entry is free for children. Bring a passport or student card as proof of your age.
Senior Citizens Many senior citizens come to the Algarve for the winter months, attracted by warm weather, a low cost of living and heavily discounted low-season long-stay rates. Ask travel agents specialising in Portugal for details.

CLOTHING SIZES

Portugal	UK	Rest of Europe	USA	
46	36	46	36	
48	38	48	38	
50	40	50	40	Suits
52	42	52	42	
54	44	54	44	
56	46	56	46	
41	7	41	8	
42	7.5	42	8.5	
43	8.5	43	9.5	Shoes
44	9.5	44	10.5	
45	10.5	45	11.5	
46	11	46	12	
37	14.5	37	14.5	
38	15	38	15	
39/40	15.5	39/40	15.5	Shirts
41	16	41	16	
42	16.5	42	16.5	
43	17	43	17	
36	8	34	6	
38	10	36	8	
40	12	38	10	Dresses
42	14	40	12	
44	16	42	14	
46	18	44	16	
38	4.5	38	6	
38	5	38	6.5	
39	5.5	39	7	Shoes
39	6	39	7.5	
40	6.5	40	8	
41	7	41	8.5	

WHEN DEPARTING

- Faro airport is small and does not have expansive shopping facilities, so do your shopping before you depart.
- Arrive at the airport no later than one hour before departing, but arrive two hours before if you want to secure a window or non-smoking seat.

LANGUAGE

The language of the Algarve is Portuguese, but most hoteliers, shopkeepers and restaurateurs also speak English and German. Portuguese is easy to understand in its written form if you already know a Romance language – such as French, Italian or Spanish. When pronounced, however, it could easily be mistaken for a Slavic language. Two sounds are distinctive to Portuguese: vowels accented with a tilda sound like *owoo* (so bread, *pão*, is pronounced *powoo*) and the s and z, which are pronounced *zsh* (so *notas*, banknotes, is pronounced *notazsh*).

hotel	*hotel/estalagem*	a double room	*quarto de casal*
do you have a room?	*tem um quarto livre?*	a twin room	*quarto com duas camas*
I have a reservation	*tenho um quarto reservado*	with bathroom	*com banho*
		one night	*um noite*
how much per night?	*qual e o preço por noite?*	key	*chave*
		sea view	*vista a mar*
a single room	*um quarto simples*	gents/ladies	*senhores/senhora*

bank	*banco*	pounds/dollars	*libras/dólares*
exchange	*office câmbios*	do you take?	*aceitam?*
post office	*correio*	credit card	*cartão de crédito*
coins	*moedas*	travellers' cheque	*cheque de viagem*
banknotes	*notas*		
receipt	*recibo*	cheque	*cheque*
the change	*troco*	how much?	*quanto custa?*
can you change?	*pode trocar?*		

breakfast	*pequeno almoço*	beer	*cerveja*
lunch	*almoço*	menu	*lista*
dinner	*jantar*	red wine	*vinho tinto*
table	*uma mesa*	white wine	*vinho branco*
starter	*entrada*	water	*água*
main course	*prato principal*	tea	*chá*
dessert	*sobremesa*	coffee (black)	*um bica*
bill	*conta*	coffee (white)	*café con leite*

airport	*aeroporto*	which way to?	*como se vai para?*
bus	*autocarro*	how far?	*a que distância?*
bus station	*estação de autocarro*	where is?	*onde está*
		car	*carro*
bus stop	*paragem*	petrol	*gasolina*
a ticket to	*um bilhete para*	petrol station	*posta de gasolina*
single	*ida*		
return	*ida e volta*		

yes	*sim*	good evening/ night	*boa noite*
no	*não*		
please	*por favor*	excuse me	*desculpe*
thank you (male)	*obrigado*	you're welcome	*está bem*
thank you (female)	*obrigada*	not at all	*de nada*
hello	*olá*	how are you?	*como está?*
goodbye	*adeus*	well, thank you	*bem, obrigado (a)*
good morning	*bom dia*	do you speak English?	*fala inglês?*
good afternoon	*bom tarde*	I don't understand	*não conpreendo*

INDEX

INDEX

Acknowledgements

The Automobile Association wishes to thank the following photographers and libraries for their assistance in the preparation of this book.

ANDALUCIA SLIDE LIBRARY (M CHAPLOW) 15b, 51b, 54c, 55c, 86b, 91a, 92/116, 122c;
MARY EVANS PICTURE LIBRARY 11b, 14b;
HULTON GETTY 11c;
MRI BANKERS' GUIDE TO FOREIGN CURRENCY 119
NATURE PHOTOGRAPHERS LTD 73b (S C Bisserott);
PICTURES COLOUR LIBRARY LTD 70/1;
POWERSTOCK/ZEFA F/Cover a (woman in traditional costume);

All remaining pictures are held in the Association's own library (AA PHOTO LIBRARY) and were taken by Michelle Chaplow with the exception of the following: M Birkitt 23b, 24b, 42, 59b; J Edmanson F/Cover b (Armacao de Pera), B/Cover, 6b, 19b, 21b, 37b, 37c, 39b, 39c, 46b, 47, 55b, 60, 74b, 88b; A Kouprianoff F/Cover a (Silves Castle), 5a, 6a, 7a, 8a, 8/9, 9a, 9c, 10a, 10b, 11a, 12a, 12b, 13a, 14a, 15a, 16a, 17a, 18a, 18b, 19a, 20a, 20b, 21a, 22a, 23a, 24a, 25a, 26a, 32b, 34, 52b, 62, 66b, 89b; P Wilson F/Cover d (tiles), 2

Editor: Jane Gregory   Page Layout: Jo Tapper

Dear Essential Traveller

Your comments, opinions and recommendations are very important to us. So please help us to improve our travel guides by taking a few minutes to complete this simple questionnaire.

You do not need a stamp (unless posted outside the UK). If you do not want to cut this page from your guide, then photocopy it or write your answers on a plain sheet of paper.

Send to: **The Editor, AA World Travel Guides, FREEPOST SCE 4598, Basingstoke RG21 4GY.**

Your recommendations…

We always encourage readers' recommendations for restaurants, nightlife or shopping – if your recommendation is used in the next edition of the guide, we will send you a *FREE* AA *Essential* **Guide** of your choice. Please state below the establishment name, location and your reasons for recommending it.

_____

_____

_____

_____

Please send me **AA *Essential*** _____

(*see list of titles inside the front cover*)

About this guide…

Which title did you buy?

AA *Essential* _____

Where did you buy it? _____

When? m m / y y

Why did you choose an AA *Essential* Guide? _____

_____

_____

_____

_____

Did this guide meet your expectations?

Exceeded ☐   Met all ☐   Met most ☐   Fell below ☐

Please give your reasons _____

_____

_____

_____

continued on next page…

Were there any aspects of this guide that you particularly liked? _____

_____

_____

_____

Is there anything we could have done better? _____

_____

_____

_____

_____

About you…

Name (*Mr/Mrs/Ms*) _____

Address _____

_____

_____ Postcode _____

Daytime tel nos _____

Which age group are you in?
Under 25 ☐ 25–34 ☐ 35–44 ☐ 45–54 ☐ 55–64 ☐ 65+ ☐

How many trips do you make a year?
Less than one ☐ One ☐ Two ☐ Three or more ☐

Are you an AA member? Yes ☐ No ☐

About your trip…

When did you book? m m / y y   When did you travel? m m / y y

How long did you stay? _____

Was it for business or leisure? _____

Did you buy any other travel guides for your trip?
If yes, which ones? _____

_____

Thank you for taking the time to complete this questionnaire. Please send
it to us as soon as possible, and remember, you do not need a stamp
(*unless posted outside the UK*).

Happy Holidays!